Ashamed of Joseph

Mormon Foundations Crumble

Ashamed of Joseph

Mormon Foundations Crumble

Charles A. Crane
&
Steven A. Crane

 COLLEGE PRESS
PUBLISHING COMPANY
Joplin, Missouri

Library of Congress Catalog Card Number: 93-71346
International Standard Book Number: 0-89900-615-9

Permissions

Scripture quotations are taken from the New American Standard Bible, ©1960, 1962, 1963, 1968, 1971, 1972, 1973, 1975, 1977 by The Lockman Foundation. Used by permission.

The *Salt Lake Tribune* has given permission to quote various news articles and advertisements gathered over several years.

Modern Microfilm Company, Box 1884, Salt Lake City, Utah 84110 has graciously given permission to quote from their many different publications and books.

Many of the primary works of the L.D.S. church are no longer under copyright but are in public domain. Several of their works that are under copyright have been quoted by permission of the Church of Jesus Christ of Latter-day Saints.

The writings of Joseph Fielding Smith have been quoted by permission of Bookcraft of Salt Lake City, Utah.

Most of the quotations in this book do not require permission because the works are either in the public domain or have been quoted within the rules of public access. We do, however, appreciate the efforts of so many scholars who have shed light on the life and work of Joseph Smith, Junior.

The cartoons are the work of Keefe Chamberlain, student at Boise Bible College.

Dedication

This book is dedicated
to Singleton Gardner Edwards

Born: February 6, 1904
Died: April 22, 1992

A wonderful Stepfather
and Grandfather,
And a mighty man of God.

Contents

Introduction

After forty years of observation and research on the subject of the Mormon church I continue to be amazed at its rapid spread. In the year 1900 there were only 250,000 members. Today an estimated eight million claim this as their church.

Traveling across the United States (as well as in numerous foreign countries), one can observe magnificent new temples, immaculately kept stake buildings, and well groomed and maintained ward buildings. These and other evidences clearly demonstrate that this religious system is growing rapidly and prospering.

As a student of the subject I have often pondered this phenomenon. With such colossal historical and doctrinal problems that have plagued them from their very beginning, how have they achieved such tremendous growth? Certainly there must be reasons.

GROWTH FACTORS

There appear to be several growth factors within the Mormon church. Many of these serve as good examples from which we could well profit. The following are a few of these factors:

1. They put everyone to work. The Mormons have an estimated 3,000 possible jobs that they assign to members.

2. They have a system of rewards or advancements of position for those who serve well.

3. Mormonism is a family-oriented religion that places a strong emphasis on marriage and children. Their emphasis on large families brings about internal growth. This growth is sometimes referred to as biological church growth.

4. Strong missionary efforts challenge their best young men and women (some not so young), to give up two years of their lives in voluntary service.[1] These recruits travel world-wide promoting the cause of Mormonism.

5. Their emphasis on tithing has given them an abundance of money to advertise and expand their work.

6. Akin to this, few who work for the church are paid. This leaves the bulk of the tithe for investments; in buildings and increasing the church's wealth. Today this wealth is compounding at an enormous rate.

7. Mormons have a vast business network; reportedly one of the largest in America. This network is able to support their expansion and mission endeavor.

8. From birth, Mormons are told that they are special

---

[1] While these terms have fluctuated, men currently serve two years while women serve eighteen months.

people because they are L.D.S. This point is drilled into them from an early age and it results in an inherent feeling of superiority and loyalty. On several occasions I have had Mormons express their sympathy for me because I am not one of "the elect."

The growth of Mormonism has also been augmented by the dereliction of duty on the part of evangelical Christians, Protestants, and even Catholics. These bodies have, too often, sat idly by while the Mormons have made vast inroads into the ranks of their religious movements. This must not continue.

We now face the prospect that in the next eighty years the Mormons may become (if their projections are correct) one of the top two or three religious movements in the world. We can no longer ignore them. We must (if we believe in Jesus Christ) take a stand and become informed about this movement. We must become lovingly militant. The Mormons will continue to increase their work force drastically.

Those of us who believe in the truth of the Bible, Jesus Christ, the judgment, eternity, heaven and hell, recognize the gigantic tragedy of those who are led by religious blind guides. We are dealing with the eternal destinies of people. We must champion truth in love.

Most churches are not prepared to combat false religious systems. Many just turn their backs when one of their members are being taught falsehood. This cannot continue.

Why must we get involved? The Mormon religion is

based on blatant errors, easily discovered hoaxes, and gross doctrinal delusions that should not be allowed to go undetected. There are few (if any) other religious systems that can so easily be demonstrated to be riddled with error.

MORMON DELUSIONS

Even much of what Mormons market to the public is not genuine. For example:

1. Their emphasis on family appears good on the surface. But in actual practice in the church it is often another thing. A good Mormon man, involved in all of the covenants of the church, working his way to the Celestial glory, is so busy his wife and family are neglected. A high-ranking friend in the Mormon church said he spent an average of twenty-seven hours a week working for the church. This was in addition to a job where he worked fifty hours. The result was a very neglected and unhappy family.

2. The Mormon "tithe" is also misunderstood. Tithing (giving ten percent of your income to the church), is only the beginning. A good Mormon family will pay up to twenty-seven percent of their income in support of necessary church programs. This straps the family financially and often makes it necessary for both husband and wife to be wage earners.

3. Although the L.D.S. system has a surface appearance of being "the restored church," underneath is a doctrine of works salvation. Initially this may have an appearance of biblical support—Christians are to produce proper works and obey Christ. But in actual practice one can never, never, ever be good enough or work hard enough to earn salvation. It is impossible for anyone to work his way to "godhood." Their best efforts leave them short of the goal. The result (to the more perceptive Mormon) is despair. For this reason there is a high level of depression among Mormon people. Suicide is disproportionately high among Mormons, and especially teens, in Utah.[2]

---

[2] This information is given in a Mormon documentary movie called *The Godmakers*, produced by Jeremiah Productions of Hollywood, CA.

An article in *The Denver Post* by John Farrell says, "Utah's divorce rate has been higher than the national average . . .and 20 is the most common age for women in Utah to get divorced . . . Utah's Child murder rate is five times the national average . . . Half of all babies born in Utah have teenage mothers and seven out of ten are conceived out of wedlock . . . But [with] the fierce pressure to remain 'respectable' in Utah, seven months has become the most common interval between marriage and child birth" (Utah: Inside the Church State, Special Reprint, Sunday Supplement, November 21-28, 1982, p. 10).

". . . Suicide is the third-highest cause of death in Utah, and teen suicide is consistently above the national average. Wife beating and child abuse are serious problems . . . Salt Lake City has twice as many reported rapes as other cities its size across America" (*Los Angeles Times*, June 26, 1983, part 1, p. 25).

4. Also worrisome is the Mormon doctrine that people who were noble in their preexistence are born into especially good stations of life. Those who were not "valiant" in their preexistence are born to lower conditions and standings. This leaves the person lacking in physical beauty or natural talent with another mountain to climb—the stigma of having been less than noble in their pre-life. All of us have shortcomings. To believe our failures were caused because we were "not valiant" in the preexistence is not only unfair, it is untrue.

Many other examples could be given, but the point should be clear. Each false doctrine carries with it a corresponding evil in the lives of those who accept it. Just as dirty water, air, or food hurt people, so does false doctrine.

Therefore, it is well past time that Christians everywhere become informed of the true nature and underpinnings of this religious system and their efforts to deceive the public concerning their true history and teachings.

You must be informed! My prayer is that this book will help you be prepared to give an answer for your faith. Today, as in past generations, the Mormon system stands or falls on the testimony of Joseph Smith. The purpose of this book is to clearly and concisely show, beyond a shadow of a doubt, that Joseph Smith was not a prophet of God! The Mormon church has every right to feel embarrassed about Joseph Smith's life and teachings. Won't you come along with us now to see why this is so.

Charles A.Crane
Steven A. Crane

ASHAMED OF JOSEPH

*Also it will come
about in that day
that the prophets
will each be ashamed
of his vision
when he prophesies . . . .*

Zechariah 13:4

CHAPTER ONE

"Sort of Embarrassed"

WHY HAS THE MORMON CHURCH BECOME "ASHAMED OF JOSEPH?"

A few months ago, the singing group from our college was invited to minister in Salt Lake City, Utah. It was my wife's and my pleasure to travel with them and for me to speak at the morning services of a local church.

Since we were in Salt Lake City, we felt it was a good time to introduce the students to the L.D.S. Visitor's Center at Temple Square. We went on that Sunday afternoon. Having lived in Salt Lake City in the 1960's and 1970's we were surprised at the major changes that had taken place in the Temple tour since those years.

Before this trip, our most recent visit had been in 1973. In days gone by a central theme that ran through the tour had been the life and teachings of Joseph Smith. In the Visitor's Center were several large paintings about him and his work; in the courtyard stood two large statues of Joseph and his brother Hiram, and the tour concluded at a large, glassed in area with Joseph in life-size diorama receiving the first vision.

This day, however, there was not one word mentioned about Joseph Smith. We were not taken to his statue; the large paintings were gone; and the diorama of Joseph receiving his first vision had vanished (it had been transformed into a meeting room). The whole impact of the tour was to leave one believing that this was a mainstream evangelical church.

This prompted me to ask several questions of the young lady who was our guide. She was gracious, lovely, and did everything she could to be helpful.

My first questions were focused primarily on the Mormon scripture and their doctrine of God. The answers were pretty standard for L.D.S. teaching.

But when I began to ask questions about Joseph Smith, she seemed reticent to answer. Finally, I pressed her to tell why nothing was said about their founding prophet during the whole length of the tour.

Her reply shocked us! "We are told to not talk about Joseph Smith."

I thought to myself, "They are not to mention the very founder and prophet of the Mormon church!" I asked, "Why?"

She replied, "We are sort of embarrassed by him today."

Again, I thought to myself, "They are ashamed of Joseph Smith, and well they should be."

A CHURCH AT A CROSSROAD

A recent *U.S. News & World Report* article is entitled, "LATTER-DAY STRUGGLES, The prosperous Mormon Church is at a theological crossroad."[3] The article says the L.D.S. religion was only an oddity found in the Inter-mountain West until recently. Its teachings were considered heterodox, tinged by violence and polygamy, and could only be considered on the fringe of orthodox Christianity.

Today, however, the church is one of the richest and fastest growing religions. The Mormons have shown unbelievable growth in recent years. A 1992 estimate claims that the Mormon church has 8.3 million members worldwide.[4] Mormons project that they will be the largest "Christian" religion, other than the Roman Catholic, by the year 2080.

Not only have they experienced dramatic numerical growth, but the Mormon empire is growing financially as well. Their annual income, according to *U.S. News & World Report*, is estimated at 4.7 billion dollars.[5]

This growth has produced political and doctrinal stresses that have prompted the Mormons to cover up their prior history and render them an appearance more

---

[3] *U.S. News & World Report*, September 28, 1992.

[4] Some, including this writer, feel membership figures are grossly overstated. There is evidence to support this view.

[5] *U.S. News & World Report*, September 28, 1992.

in line with mainstream Christianity.

In doing this, many issues have become battle-grounds — some rather public, others behind the scenes, and most only realized by those who live in the inner circle of Utah.

Some prominent issues include: the place of women in the family and church, the doctrine of black Africans, the practice of polygamy, and the use of alcoholic drinks, coffee, tea and other drinks containing caffeine. Other current issues focus on the various Mormon scriptures as to which are most authoritative. Are Mormons bound primarily by the teachings of the Bible, the *Book of Mormon*, the *Doctrine and Covenants*, or the *Pearl of Great Price?*

The Mormons have diligently worked at changing their image from "bizarre" to mainstream Christianity. They realize that in order to accomplish this feat, they will have to drastically change their appearance.[6]

The L.D.S. church has been one of the most successful modern religious bodies to adapt themselves to Liberal Democratic Capitalism. To accomplish their objectives, they have thrown in a big measure of business and prosperity, along with apple pie, baseball, and of course

---

[6] In recent years the L.D.S. church has initiated a powerful campaign to persuade people that Mormonism is a Christian religion. Television and newspaper advertisements proclaim that Mormons believe that Jesus Christ is Lord and Savior. They speak of the "Church of Jesus Christ of Latter-day Saints."These advertisements have been highly successful. If you don't realize the extent of their advertisements, pick up a *Readers Digest* or a *TV Guide*. Better yet, sit down and watch a TV show during prime time.

the all important imagery of the Mormon family.

This is all served up in a modern package that is diametrically opposed to their beginning. In order to make this chameleon type of change the Mormons have had to de-emphasize the very things that were their main themes a few years ago.

It is safe to say that their emphasis of Joseph Smith is one of the areas in which they are making a radical shift. Much of what Joseph Smith did, said, or wrote, and even who he was, is repugnant to them—as it would be to most thinking people.

Herein lies the proposition of this book—what has caused the Mormon church to de-emphasize the role of their founder and prophet? Why is the Church of Jesus Christ of Latter-day Saints "ashamed of Joseph?"

CHAPTER TWO

Accepting the Challenge

The era in which we live today could be called the age of "Religious Relativism." When dealing with the issues of Mormonism, I have often heard views expressed that go something like this: "If people are sincere, leave them alone," or, "They are not hurting anyone—so why should we care?"

If one believes very little, these arguments may sound logical. But for those people who believe in absolutes (such things as truth and error, right and wrong, God and the Devil, good and evil) to be silent is not only cowardice, but a gross neglect of one's spiritual and eternal duty.

For people of principle, religious claims are vitally

important—as important as clean water, healthful food, good medical care, and a high quality of education. What people believe is of vital importance because it directly affects their actions and will determine their eternal destiny.

For the logically oriented thinking person, the challenge of Mormonism should be accepted. The Mormons challenge us to "seek and pray to see if what we teach is true." We will prayerfully examine the evidence to "see whether they are from God."[7]

This book stems not out of ill will or from a desire for controversy, but from a deep love for people in general and concern for Mormons in particular. It comes from realizing the eternal value of every soul. Our primary motive is love—a love for people and a love of truth.

How to Approach the Subject

A word of caution seems appropriate here. Paul, the Apostle of Christ, wrote, "Knowledge makes arrogant, but love edifies."[8] We must be careful that our study be for the purpose of building people up, not putting them down.

It is only an attitude of love that gives us the right to speak with a Mormon neighbor or friend. If love does not shine through this book, then it will do little lasting good.

Often even truth spoken in love can initially be offen-

---

[7] 1 John 4:1
[8] 1 Corinthians 8:1

sive. If we do not speak in love they will not respond. If we speak in love, they may initially be offended, but later come to realize the truth. Our goal must be to share truth in love with the hope that we are able to start a person on the path to clear thinking. To start a person thinking can have dramatic results.

It will take more than a minimal effort on our part to be prepared to help our L.D.S. friends, and in trying to help we must always remember that information without love is dead.

To effectively champion truth and lead people to Christ a person will need to exhibit the following characteristics in their life:

1. Godliness. You must completely surrender your life to Christ and be willing to be used by Him.
2. Prayer. Trust that God will indeed use your life to reach others.
3. Friendship. Only your genuine friendship and concern for a person gives you the right to speak to them.
4. Patience. It is dangerous to share too much too soon. It can be offensive to come on too strong. Design your discussions to help them think and allow them the time and opportunity to consider what has been said. When a person starts thinking logically, they are on their way out of Mormonism and are on their way to biblical Christianity.
5. Truth. We are all in search of truth. Be careful to maintain an open mind at all times. Learn and

grow with your Mormon friends. Help and encourage them to grow with you. L.D.S. people are not the enemy, but victims of our mutual enemy—the father of lies, the Devil.

In reading this book, you will discover many good reasons why The Church of Jesus Christ of Latter-day Saints has become ashamed of Joseph Smith. The purpose of this book is not to be conclusive, but to survey some of the more pressing issues that affect the credibility of their founding prophet, Joseph Smith, Jr.[9]

---

[9] Referred to from this point onward as Joseph Smith.

CHAPTER THREE

An Encounter with Joseph Smith

One day a very handsome, strong man of obvious intelligence came to our door. My first impression was that I had met him somewhere before, but I couldn't quite place him.

He offered his hand and introduced himself saying, "My name is Joseph Smith and I am a direct descendant of the Prophet Joseph Smith." It immediately became clear why I felt I knew him. He bore a remarkable resemblance to his great-great grandfather, Joseph Smith.

You can imagine my feeling—he so resembled his forbearer that the likeness was uncanny. In just a short time, one thing became immediately clear; this man in front of me was no one's dummy. He was cultured, bright eyed, and seemed to be a remarkable human being. I immediately liked him.

But something puzzled me. Why was the great-great-grandson of Joseph Smith at my door? I soon discovered that he had read my book, *The Bible and Mormon Scriptures Compared* and wished to discuss some of my conclusions and address current Utah Branch, L.D.S. teachings. We entered into a study that took place several times.

We discussed Mormon scripture, Mormon doctrine, the various splits that had taken place in the L.D.S. movement, and other items that were upon his mind. My appreciation of this man increased greatly during the time we spent together.

I found him bright, open-minded, cordial and ready to learn. But most importantly, he taught me a great many things that I did not know. You might find it interesting he was not Utah Branch Mormon, or a Reorganized Mormon, but was a Hedrickite (a small, splinter group that still owns the Temple Lot property in Independence, Missouri).[10]

He, understandably, was quick to defend his ancestor whom he considered to be a prophet, but did not accept many of the teachings of mainstream Mormonism today, nor the history as it has often been written or rewritten.

He affirmed that there had been a very strong and

---

[10] He would claim that they are the true successors of the prophet.

clear oral transmission of information through his family. He had received his information from his father, who had in turn received it from his father, and so on back to Joseph Smith.

The main benefit I received from our discussions came in learning about Joseph Smith. He was not a wacko, or a half-wit as some would depict him, but was an extraordinary human being of great physical strength, intellectual endowments, and outstanding personality traits.

These discussions brought to my mind a conversation from the past. Years ago I talked with a man named Larry Jonas, a scholar of Mormonism, who held similar views of Joseph Smith. He claimed that Joseph Smith was no one's fool, but rather was a man of inestimable natural gifts, probably a genius.

This in part explains why he was able to accomplish many of the things that fall to his credit. It is true that he had only a meager public education (about the eighth grade in school), but genius is not taught; it comes as a natural gift. One must submit that his accomplishments were a remarkable feat for such a short lifetime.

I now believe that Joseph Smith was a genius. But I also believe that he was a misguided genius. A similar attitude is held among many L.D.S. people when they learn the truth about Joseph Smith.

Joseph was strong of body, quick of mind, with a strong and charismatic personality. He was very convincing, capable of leading people, had a very quick wit and was exceptionally cunning. Because of these traits, he was able to begin a religious movement that has become one of the strongest ever started in America.

Joseph's life and work are parallel in many ways to Mohammed, another religious prophet.

Mohammed was born at Mecca, August 20, 570 and died at the age of sixty-two at Medina.[11] Because of the early deaths of his mother and father, and due to the fact that he was passed from person to person, he did not receive much of an education. Some say that he never even learned to read or write. Yet, he was able to unite several political factions and become the leader of what has become one of the major religions in the world today.

The similarities are numerous. Both Joseph and Mohammed had an unsettled and traumatic early life. Both men lacked significant education. Both claimed to have a religious experience that they claimed set them apart for a special work for God. Both men loved many women and practiced polygamy. Both men entered into sexual union with very young girls. Both men had war-like tendencies. Both men claimed supernatural communication with God. Both men were very evangelistic in spreading their beliefs and both gave a book that is claimed to be scripture (the *Koran* and the *Book of Mormon*). Both men based their new religious systems on the Old and New Testaments.

This is only a very brief comparison, but they go on and on until one must feel that they have been motivated by the same source. What is that source? We must examine the information and learn why the Latter-day Saints are growing more and more ashamed of Joseph.

Always remember, though, that we are not dealing with an ordinary person, but a person with outstanding

---

[11] See the *New Schaff-Herzog Encyclopedia of Religious Knowledge*, Vol. VII, pp. 436 ff.

natural gifts. Joseph Smith could well be described as a very intelligent man.

CHAPTER FOUR

An Embarrassing Dilemma

There are many reasons why the Mormon church is ashamed of Joseph Smith. The defenders of Mormonism have spent over a century and a half trying to defend Joseph Smith with little success. In fact, their scholars have had the proverbial "egg on their face" so often simply because of who he was, what he did, and what he taught—to the point that many Mormon leaders have grown weary of trying to defend him.

It is not suggested that every Mormon feels this way about Joseph Smith nor that this is the official church position; only that it is readily apparent that their policy is now to de-emphasize their founding prophet—and for very good reason.

You can't really blame them for their new approach.

It has been a long time in coming—too long! It is time for everyone to realize the true character of Joseph Smith. This new approach has serious implications for their whole movement.

Again, I am not suggesting that every Mormon is ashamed of Joseph Smith, or even that this feeling is widespread. I am, however, suggesting that the Mormon church realizes that to stress Joseph Smith is to continually have to defend what cannot be defended.

In the past, the L.D.S. church has taught that Joseph Smith was next to Jesus himself; some have even taught that he was better than Jesus. Brigham Young said August 13, 1871 in the New Tabernacle in Salt Lake City:

> Well, now examine the character of the Savior, and examine the character of those who have written the Old and New Testament; and then compare them with the character of Joseph Smith, the founder of this work . . . and you will find that his character stands as fair as that of any man's mentioned in the Bible. We can find no person who presents a better character to the world when the facts are known than Joseph Smith, Jun., the prophet . . . .[12]

THEIR CHALLENGE ACCEPTED

We would like to accept this challenge of Brigham Young—to examine the character of Joseph Smith and compare it to that of Jesus Christ! Can Joseph really measure up to the standard set by the Son of God?

Brigham Young suggested that Joseph Smith could more than measure up:

> . . . A better man never lived upon the face of the earth.[13]

---

[12] *Journal of Discourses*, Vol.14, p. 203.
[13] *Journal of Discourses*, Vol. 4, p. 41.

According to Mormon teaching, it is Joseph who is currently working on behalf of mankind and it is Joseph who will give the consent necessary for a man to enter into the heavenly realms.

> . . . no man or woman in this dispensation will ever enter into the celestial kingdom of God without the consent of Joseph Smith . . . Every man and woman must have the certificate of Joseph Smith, Junior, as a passport to their entrance into the mansion where God and Christ are . . . I cannot go there without his consent . . . He reigns there as supreme a being in his sphere, capacity, and calling, as God does in heaven.[14]

Mormon teaching goes on to say that Joseph Smith in no uncertain terms is a "god" to this world!

> He is the man through whom God has spoken . . . yet I would not like to call him a savior, though in a certain capacity he was a God to us, and is to the nations of the earth, and will continue to be.[15]

On one occasion Joseph Smith declared,

> I have more to boast of than ever any man had. I am the only man who has ever been able to keep a whole church together since the days of Adam . . . Neither Paul, John, Peter, nor Jesus ever did it. I boast that no man ever did such a work as I.[16]

Joseph Smith also said, "I am learned and know more than all the world put together.[17] Smith boasted that he

---

[14] *Journal of Discourses*, Vol. 7, p. 289.

[15] *Journal of Discourses*, Vol. 8, p. 321.

[16] Joseph Smith, *History of the Church*, Vol. 6, pp. 408-409.

[17] Joseph Fielding Smith, *Teachings of the Prophet Joseph Smith*, p. 350.

alone could comprehend "heaven, earth, and hell" and that God himself was his "right-hand man."[18]

The sixth president of the Mormon church, Joseph F. Smith, stated that

> Joseph Smith's name will never perish, and that his name will be held in reverence and honor among men as universally as the name of Jesus Christ.[19]

As stated previously, the new approach of the Mormon church to de-emphasize Joseph Smith has serious implications for the whole movement. Their claim has been that Joseph Smith translated the *Book of Mormon*. It is Joseph who gave most of the revelations in the *Doctrine and Covenants*. He is the one who translated the *Book of Abraham* in the *Pearl of Great Price*. It is Joseph who made an estimated 4,000 changes in the Bible in his *Inspired Version*. It is Joseph Smith in the eyes of the Mormons who established the "only true church on earth."

Joseph Fielding Smith, the tenth prophet and president of the Mormon church said that there is

> . . . no salvation without accepting Joseph Smith. If Joseph Smith was verily a prophet, and if he told the truth . . . then this knowledge is of the most vital importance to the entire world. No man can reject that testimony without incurring the most dreadful consequences, for he cannot enter the Kingdom of God.

---

[18] Joseph Smith, *History of the Church of Jesus Christ of Latter-day Saints*, Vol. 5, p. 209 and Vol.6, pp. 408-409.

[19] Joseph F. Smith, *Gospel Doctrine: Selections from the Sermons and Writings of Joseph F. Smith*, p. 479.

Again Joseph Fielding Smith said:

Mormonism, as it is called, must stand or fall on the story of Joseph Smith. He was either a prophet of God, divinely called, properly appointed and commissioned, or he was one of the biggest frauds this world has ever seen. There is no middle ground.

If Joseph Smith was a deceiver, who wilfully attempted to mislead the people, then he should be exposed; his claims should be refuted, and his doctrines shown to be false, for the doctrines of an imposter cannot be made to harmonize in all particulars with divine truth. If his claims and declarations were built upon fraud and deceit, there would appear many errors and contradictions, which would be easy to detect. The doctrines of false teachers will not stand the test when tried by the accepted standards of measurement, the Scriptures.[20]

For them to be ashamed of Joseph Smith is to admit that the whole foundation of their church is built upon a *man* and not God. To prove Joseph Smith a liar is to prove Mormonism a hoax.

The Mormons realize this and have found themselves in an embarrassing dilemma. If they downplay the role of Joseph Smith in an attempt to appear more Christian, they leave behind the very roots and foundation upon which they were built. If they uphold Joseph Smith as their founder and prophet they must continue the futile attempt to defend what cannot be defended.

The following chapters will give a glimpse into why the Mormon church is "ashamed of Joseph."

---

[20] *Doctrines of Salvation*, 1:188.

ASHAMED OF HIS CHARACTER

Well, now examine the character
of the Savior, and examine the character
of those who have written the Old and New Testament;
and then compare them with the character
of Joseph Smith, the founder of this work . . .
and you will find that his character stands
as fair as that of any man's mentioned in
the Bible. We can find no person who presents
a better character to the world when
the facts are known than
Joseph Smith, Jun., the prophet . . . .

Journal of Discourses, Vol. 14, p. 203.

CHAPTER FIVE

The Character of Joseph Smith

There are many reasons why the L.D.S. church should be ashamed of Joseph Smith. A primary reason is found in his character.

When Jesus stood before Pilate there had been many accusations brought against Him. Some people were saying that He was misleading the nation. Others were claiming that He was refusing to pay taxes to Caesar. Some were calling Him an insurrectionist. Still others called Him a blasphemer. But Pilate (the equivalent to our appellate court judge) said, "I have found no fault in this man."[21] This verdict still rings true today. There can be found no fault in Jesus Christ.

---

[21] Luke 23:14

When Paul spoke of Jesus Christ and what He did for mankind, he could passionately say, "For I am not ashamed of the gospel . . . ."[22]

Mormons, however, are ashamed of Joseph Smith's personal history. It is only possible to give a brief summary of what can be said, but suffice it to say that over 60% of his history was written after he died, and these accounts are not at all accurate.

In their book, *The Changing World of Mormonism*, Jerald and Sandra Tanner demonstrate that Mormon historians have changed much of Joseph's history. Mormon leaders have changed the very writing of their prophet. They, and not Joseph Smith, are the ones who completed the majority of the *History of the Church* which is said to be "his history." In completing this work, they have deleted important material and have given falsified accounts of his life.

The Tanners provide irrefutable evidence that these altered accounts provide an unrealistic view of the life and teachings of Joseph Smith. In the process of completing his history, church historians removed and changed many of Smith's writings; they alleviated profanities; deleted falsified information; and wrote unrealistic accounts of his life. The following is a quote from the Tanners' book:

> Mormon historians have also changed some of Joseph Smith's prophecies that did not come to pass. Many exaggerated and contradictory statements were either changed or deleted without indication. Crude or indecent statements were also deleted. Joseph Smith quoted the enemies of the church as using the name of the Lord

---

[22] Romans 1:16

in vain many times in the history, but much of this pro-
fanity has been removed by Mormon leaders. In the first
printed version of Joseph Smith's history he cursed his
enemies, condemned other churches and beliefs, and
called the President of the United States a fool. Many of
these extreme statements were omitted or changed.
Mormon leaders did not dare let their people see the
real Joseph Smith. They would rather falsify the *History
of the Church* than allow Joseph Smith's true character to
be known.[23] Mormon leaders have not only changed the
History of the Church, but they have further deceived
their people by making the claim that no historical or
doctrinal statement has been changed.

Not only has the *History of the Church* been changed
since it was first printed, but there is also evidence to
prove that changes were made before it was first published. In other words, there is evidence that even the
first printed version of the history is inaccurate. It does
not agree with the handwritten manuscript.[24]

The Mormons have gone to great lengths to cover up
the true history of Joseph Smith. The Tanners conclude
their discussion of the history of Joseph Smith by saying:

Less than forty percent of the history attributed to
Joseph Smith was written during his lifetime, and this
portion has had serious changes made in it. The remain-
ing portion—more than sixty percent of the history —
was not even compiled until after Joseph Smith's death.
Since it was compiled by men who believed in falsifica-
tion and deceit, it cannot be trusted as a reliable history
of Joseph Smith.[25]

---

[23] Italics mine.
[24] Jerald and Sandra Tanner, *The Changing World of Mormonism*, p. 399.
[25]*Ibid.*, p. 415.

Why has there been such a blatant attempt to hide Joseph Smith's history? Because Mormon leaders dare not show the true colors of their founding prophet! A person needs only look at the history of Joseph Smith to realize that he is in no way a prophet. Let's turn our attention to Joseph Smith to ascertain whether or not he really was a man of God.

CHAPTER SIX

The Glass Looker

It has been well publicized that in his younger years, Joseph spent much of his time looking for buried treasure. Joseph Smith's own father-in-law testifies to the fact that he was a glass looker.

I first became acquainted with Joseph Smith, Jr. in November, 1825. He was at that time in the employ of a set of men who were called "money diggers;" and his occupation was that of seeing, or pretending to see by means of a stone placed in his hat, and his hat closed over his face. In this way he pretended to discover minerals and hidden treasures. His appearance at this time, was that of a careless young man—not very well educated, and very saucy and insolent to his father. Smith, and his father, with several other "money diggers" boarded at my house while they were employed in digging for a mine that they supposed had been opened and worked by the Spaniards, many years since. Young Smith gave the "money diggers" great encouragement at first, but when they had arrived in digging, to near the place where he had stated an immense treasure would be found—he said the enchantment was so powerful that he could not see. They then became discouraged, and soon after dispersed. This took place about the 17th of November, 1825; and one of the company gave me his note for $12.68 for his board, which is still unpaid.

After these occurrences, young Smith made several visits at my house, and at length asked my consent to his marrying my daughter Emma. . . .

Issac Hale[26]

Another account which testifies to Smith being a glasslooker, was written by a contemporary of Joseph Smith and gives the following account.

We, the undersigned, have been acquainted with the Smith family, for a number of years, while they resided near this place, and we have no hesitation in saying, that we consider them destitute of that moral character, which ought to entitle them to the confidence of any community. They were particularly famous for visionary projects, spent much of their time in diggings for money which they pretended was hid in the earth; and to this day, large excavations may be seen in the earth, not far from their residence, where they used to spend their time in digging for hidden treasures. Joseph Smith, Senior, and his son Joseph, were in particular, considered entirely destitute of moral character, and addicted to vicious habits.[27]

---

[26] E.D. Howe, *Mormonism Unveiled*, pp. 262-263.
[27] *Ibid.*, p. 261.

This document was signed by Mr. Howe as well as sixty-two residents of Palmyra, New York.

While fortune seeking, in and of itself, is not illegal, fraudulent behavior is. A legal problem arose when Joseph Smith claimed that he could find buried treasure by means of a stone, accepted money in return for his abilities, and yet was unable to provide what he promised.

In 1826, Joseph Smith was brought to trial and convicted of fraudulent activity with a "peep stone." It was proven in court that Joseph Smith on numerous occasions took money in exchange for his "seer" abilities.

Mormon leaders have repeatedly tried to argue and refute these charges of questionable behavior. The Mormon church officially stated in the *Deseret News*, church Section, May 11, 1946, that the charges against Joseph Smith were forged and that Joseph Smith had never stood trial in such a case. Mormon Apostle John A. Widtsoe in dealing with this very issue stated that:

> This alleged court record . . . seems to be a literary attempt of an enemy to ridicule Joseph Smith . . . There is no existing proof that such a trial was ever held.[28]

Mormon scholars continued to deny the charges until Wesley P. Walters found an original court document in Norwich, New York —a document which is more than 165 years old. This document is positive proof of what had long been believed—that Joseph Smith was involved in money digging and other questionable practices.

---

[28] John Widtsoe, *Joseph Smith—Seeker After Truth*, p. 78.

I know Wesley P. Walters personally and have inserted here a copy of a court document showing fees assessed when Joseph Smith was tried and convicted.

This photograph, reproduced in Tanner, *Mormonism—Shadow or Reality*, is the bill of Justice Albert Neely, showing costs involved in several trials in 1826, including that of "Joseph Smith the Glass Looker." (The double "S" in "glass" appears like a "P", as also in the word "Assault" in some of the other trials.) This bill shows that the published court record is authentic. The record for Joseph Smith reads: "Same vs Joseph Smith The Glass Looker March 20, 1826 / Misdemeanor / To my fees in examination of the above cause 2.68."

Much to the dismay of Mormon leaders—there can no longer be any doubt that Joseph Smith was brought up on legal charges, and found guilty of questionable behavior.

Fraser's Magazine in 1873 gives further light to this incident in the following account:

State of New York v. Joseph Smith. Warrant issued upon written complaint upon oath of Peter G. Bridgeman, who informed that one Joseph Smith of Bainbridge was a disorderly person and impostor. Prisoner brought before Court March 20, 1826. Prisoner examined: says that he came from the town of Palmyra, and had been at the house of Josiah Stowel in Bainbridge most of time since; had small part of time been employed by said Stowel on his farm, and going to school. That he had a certain stone which he had occasionally looked at to determine where hidden treasures in the bowels of the earth were; that he professed to tell in this manner where gold mines were a distance under ground, and had looked for Mr. Stowel several times, and had informed him where he could find these treasures, and Mr. Stowel had been engaged in digging for them. That at Palmyra he pretended to tell by looking at this stone where coined money was buried in Pennsylvania, and while at Palmyra had frequently ascertained in that way where lost property was of various kinds; that he had occasionally been in the habit of looking through this stone to find lost property for three years, but of late had pretty much given it up on account of its injuring his health, especially his eyes, making them sore; that he did not solicit business of this kind, and had always rather declined having anything to do with this business.

. . . And therefore the Court finds the Defendant guilty. Costs: Warrant, 19c. Complaint upon oath, 25 1/2c. Seven witnesses, 87 1/2c. Recognizances, 25 c. Mittimus, 19c. Recognizances of witnesses, 75c. Subpoena, 18 c.- $2.68.[29]

---

[29] *Fraser's Magazine*, Feb. 1873, pp. 229-230.

Not only was Joseph tried, found guilty, and sentenced, but it is also reported that Joseph jumped bail. Joseph returned a year later claiming that the statute of limitations had run out. All this took place four years before Joseph Smith founded the Mormon church and six years after his "first revelation from God."

There is no room for doubt that Joseph Smith's glass-looking and his lying about his ability to know hidden things, is a great embarrassment to the L.D.S. church. It is a further embarrassment when one realizes that the stone which Joseph fraudulently used to hunt for buried treasure is the very type of stone by which he claims to have translated the *Book of Mormon*.[30]

It is an interesting comparison to note that Joseph Smith was tried, convicted, and then jumped bail—refusing to pay the debt that he owed. Christ on the other hand was found innocent of any transgression and yet chose to pay for a crime He didn't commit. Jesus could have called ten thousand angels to free Him from the punishment that He did not deserve, but rather chose to die in our place.

And yet, the Mormons claim, "no better man ever lived than Joseph Smith."

---

[30] Joseph Smith fastened two of his "seer stones" together to make up what he called the "Urim and Thummim."

CHAPTER SEVEN

The Story Teller

Another reason the L.D.S. should be ashamed of Joseph Smith is found when examining the "first vision." The authenticity of this vision is of vital importance because it is this event in which God supposedly conveyed to Joseph Smith that all other religions were an abomination and that he was to establish what today is referred to as the church of Jesus Christ of Latter-day Saints. The first vision is referred to by the Mormons as the "very foundation" of the church.

David O. McKay, Mormon Apostle and leader said:

> The appearing of the Father and the Son to Joseph Smith is the foundation of this Church.[31]

---

[31] David O. McKay, *Gospel Ideals*, p. 85.

John A. Widtsoe, Mormon Apostle stated it this way:

The First Vision of 1820 is of first importance in the history of Joseph Smith. Upon its reality rest the truth and value of his subsequent work.[32]

The Mormons themselves realize that the integrity of Joseph Smith and the truth of Mormonism are at stake with the reliability of the "first vision." To prove Joseph Smith and the first vision unreliable would bring a fatal blow to the very foundation of Mormonism.

The "official account" was written by Smith about 1838 and was published in 1842. Smith claimed that this vision occurred while he was living in Manchester, New York, during the time when there was a significant revival in the land. Smith was concerned because there were many divisions between the denominations. He wondered how any of these religious groups could be correct when they all came from different theological perspectives. Therefore, he prayed to God to see which, if any, of these denominations were correct. The 1842 account relates the vision as follows:

So in accordance with my determination, to ask of God, I retired to the woods to make the attempt. It was on the morning of a beautiful clear day, early in the spring of eighteen hundred and twenty . . . I saw a pillar of light exactly over my head . . . When the light rested upon me I saw two personages (whose brightness and glory defy all description) standing above me in the air. One of them spoke unto me, calling me by name, and said, (pointing to the other,) 'This is my beloved Son, hear him.' . . . I asked the personages who stood above me in the light, which of all the sects was right . . . I was

---

[32] John A. Widtsoe, *Joseph Smith-Seeker After Truth*, p. 19.

answered that I must join none of them, said that all their creeds were an abomination in his sight; that those professors were all corrupt . . . He again forbade me to join with any of them: and many other things did he say unto me which I cannot write at this time.[33]

This account is accepted as scripture by the Mormons today.

Isn't it strange that there was no mention of this foundational event by anyone until 1842? There is not one mention of this vision for over two decades after the event occurred. If, in truth, Joseph Smith had this memorable experience in 1820, it passed totally unnoticed by all for twenty-two years.[34]

Even Brigham Young, an associate of Joseph Smith—a man who had 363 of his sermons recorded in the *Journal of Discourses*, failed to mention the first vision. The historians of the Mormon church and companions of Joseph Smith, Oliver Cowdery and John Whitmer, had ample opportunity to record this event, but never refer to this incident in their writings.

In the records we have on file of Oliver Cowdery, and John Whitmer, such as they are, we do not find a reference to the First Vision.[35]

Not a single person (Joseph Smith, Brigham Young, Oliver Cowdery, John Whitmer, nor any other living person) wrote an account of this historical event during

---

[33]Joseph Smith, *Pearl of Great Price*, 2:18,19, and *Times and Seasons*, Vol. 3, pp. 728-748.

[34] See *No Man Knows my History*, pp. 24-25.

[35] Jerald Tanner, *Mormonism: A Study of Mormon History and Doctrine*, p. 79.

the first two decades after it supposedly happened.

A person cannot claim that Joseph spent twenty-two years pondering what God had said to him, and just never got around to doing anything about his vision. This two decade period included the founding of the church and the publishing of the *Book of Mormon*. These two events provided an opportune time for Joseph Smith to relate his vision—but Joseph never told anyone!

The *Book of Mormon*, the book which claims to be "another testament of the Lord Jesus Christ," was published in 1830. If the first vision was in fact a reality, wouldn't it make sense for Joseph Smith to mention the fact that God had chosen him to translate this companion scripture? Shouldn't Joseph have related the events of 1820 at this time?

The Mormon church was started in 1830. If the very founding of the church stemmed from a vision that Joseph received from God, why didn't Joseph relate the vision to the church when the church was established? It seems remiss of Joseph to forget such a major detail, if it were a real event.

If the first vision is the foundational event on which the credibility and authenticity of Joseph Smith resides, why didn't Joseph talk about his encounter when he received the second vision in 1823? Why didn't he mention it to Brigham Young? Why not tell the church historians? Don't you find it a little strange—that an event of biblical proportions was never mentioned by Joseph to anyone during a twenty-two year time frame? It certainly would be strange if the event actually happened.

CONFLICTING ACCOUNTS

Further damage is done to the credibility of the first vision when one examines the conflicting accounts of Joseph's vision. It is amazing to discover that when Joseph finally gets around to telling his story, his accounts are contradictory.

In 1966, a conflicting account of Joseph Smith's vision came to light. This is an account of the same vision we looked at earlier, written in Joseph Smith's own handwriting.

> . . . the Lord heard my cry in the wilderness and while in the attitude of calling upon the Lord in the 16th year of my age a pillar of light above the brightness of the sun at noon day came down from above and rested upon me and I was filled with the spirit of god and the Lord opened the heavens upon me and I saw the Lord and he spoke unto me saying Joseph my son thy sins are forgiven thee, go thy way walk in my statutes and keep my commandments behold I am the Lord of glory I was crucified for the world that all those who believe on my name may have Eternal life behold the world lieth in sin at this time and none doeth good no not one they have turned aside from the gospel and keep not my commandments they draw near to me with their lips while their hearts are far from me and mine anger is kindling against the inhabitants of the earth to visit them according to this ungodliness and to bring to pass that which hath been spoken by the mouth of the prophets and Apostles behold and lo I come quickly as it was w(r)itten of me in the cloud clothed in the glory of my Father.[36]

---

[36] *Brigham Young University Studies*, spring 1969 issue, p. 281.

If you were to examine these accounts closely, you would notice several discrepancies. Not only is his age different;[37] his reason for seeking God is different; only one personage appears to him; there is no revival; and now there is the presence of an evil power.

Tell me this, if you received an important message from God, would you remember some of the important details? Would you remember how old you were? Would you remember who spoke to you? Would you remember these major details two decades later? You would if it were an actual experience.

A third account of the first vision has been found as part of the Prophet's 1835-36 Diary.

> . . . I called on the Lord in mighty prayer, a pillar of fire appeared above my head, it presently rested down upon my head, and filled me with joy unspeakable, a personage appeared in the midst of the pillar of flame which was spread all around, and yet nothing consumed, another personage soon appeared like unto the first, he said unto me thy sins are forgiven thee, he testified (sic) unto me that Jesus Christ is the Son of God; and I saw many angels in this vision I was about 14 years old when I received this first communication . . . .[38]

This account again gives the age at 14 which is in harmony with the official account, but instead of one person, or two personages, many angels appear to Joseph!

---

[37] The official version of the Mormon church dates the event as happening in the spring of 1820. Joseph was born on December 23, 1805 and would have only been 14 at this time. The handwritten account, however, gives his age at sixteen.

[38] Joseph Smith's Diary, 1835-36, p. 24, as quoted in *Dialogue: A Journal of Mormon Thought*, Spring 1971, p. 87.

There is no mention here of seeing the Father or the Son. The other two accounts don't mention the fact that their were angels present, but in this account he "saw many angels." And this is not the end to the conflicting accounts. What many people do not realize is that there are at least six different accounts of the "first vision."[39] When examining these accounts, it seems more like the growth of a fish story than a real event. These dissenting accounts have been repressed by Mormon leaders due to the very fact that they disagree with the "official version."

One account depicts an angel appearing to Joseph Smith. In another account Joseph claims that Jesus appeared to him. In yet another incident, Joseph once again changes the account to suggest that the Father, Son, and Holy Ghost appeared to him. One account depicts angels and two personages. In these conflicting accounts, the age is different, the content is different, even the surrounding circumstances of these visions are different. It can even be documented that there were no revivals in New York between 1819 and 1824.[40] This in itself is detrimental to Joseph Smith and his account of the first vision. Each of these accounts is so contradictory and controversial, that it can only lead a reasonable person to believe that there never was a vision.

It also should be noted that in the official version, Joseph Smith is told not to join any sect or denomination because they are all corrupt, and yet eight years

---

[39] See Tanner and Tanner, *The Changing World of Mormonism*, for an exhaustive discussion on this matter.

[40] Wesley P. Walters, *New Light on Mormon Originals*, p. 3.

later in 1828, Joseph Smith joined a Methodist church. Joseph Smith's name remained on the church rolls until it was removed because of his questionable behavior in treasure hunting and spiritism.[41] How quickly one forgets the voice of God who said that all churches on earth were corrupt.

It is also intriguing to find that although Joseph Smith claimed to have a conversation with God or from God, in the account of his second vision of 1823, he doubts God's very existence. If Joseph spoke to God, or even to a messenger from God, shouldn't he realize that THERE IS A GOD?

Wouldn't you also expect that if Joseph Smith had an encounter with a celestial being, his lifestyle would be dramatically altered by this heavenly encounter? Even Joseph Smith admits that in the years following his first vision he lived a questionable lifestyle.

In light of this evidence, ask yourself the following questions. "Was this a real encounter with God, or is it possible that Joseph Smith fabricated the whole story?" "Did Joseph really have an encounter with God when he was fourteen or sixteen?"

Let's continue with our comparison of Joseph Smith and Jesus Christ. I remember a story of Jesus when he was near the age of fourteen (actually he was twelve). Jesus was not depicted as a mischievous young boy who went promenading about the countryside in search of buried treasure. Jesus was never accused of stealing money from the unsuspecting. Jesus was never questioned for having made up an unbelievable story. He

---

[41] See the *Amboy Journal*, April 30, 1879, and June 11, 1879.

did, however, cause a disturbance at the age of twelve. If you remember the story, Joseph and Mary were returning home from Jerusalem after the Feast of the Passover and discovered that Jesus was not with them. When they found Jesus—do you remember where he was? Jesus was in the temple talking with the scribes.

> And it came about that after three days they found Him in the temple, sitting in the midst of the teachers, both listening to them and asking them questions. And all who heard Him were amazed at His understanding and His answers.[42]

But Joseph Smith claimed of himself that no better man ever lived. Yes, it is easy to see why the Mormons are "ashamed of Joseph."

---

[42] Luke 2:46-47

CHAPTER EIGHT

A Man of Little Integrity

E. D. Howe was a contemporary of Joseph Smith and charged him with many offenses that Joseph never refuted. In a quotation we looked at earlier, Howe and sixty-two other witnesses of Palmyra, NY, testified that both Joseph Smith and his father were,

> . . . destitute of that moral character, which ought to entitle them to the confidence of any community. . . ,

and that they were,

> entirely destitute of moral character, and addicted to vicious habits.[43]

---

[43]*Mormonism Unveiled*, p. 261.

It would be easy to dismiss these words as religion bashing or rumormongering if they were not so much in agreement with the other preponderance of evidence.

History shows Joseph Smith to have been an open liar. For many years he tried to cover up the practice of polygamy—a practice that was probably started as early as 1838. When examined by the *Elder's Journal*, however, he denied this practice. When specifically asked if any of the Mormons had more than one wife, Joseph emphatically replied, "No."

He was accused by Augustine Spencer of

> drinking, swearing, carousing, dancing all night, etc., and that he keeps six or seven young females as wives . . . .[44]

He denied the practice of polygamy again in 1844.[45]

As late as 1850 John Taylor, who would later become the third president of the church, denied that the church believed in the practice of plural marriage, when he himself at the time had six living wives.

It was not until 1852 that the Mormons publicly admitted that they were practicing polygamy. Joseph had been lying about polygamy and his example was followed by the Mormon leaders that followed him.

In the 132nd section of the *Doctrine and Covenants* Joseph Smith goes to great length to justify his practice of polygamy. This was written in 1843, yet for several years he had denied the practice existed.

Fawn M. Brodie, niece of the Prophet David O. McKay, wrote a very controversial book entitled, *No Man Knows My History*. Before Joseph's death he had

---

[44] Letter by Parley P. Pratt concerning Augustine Spencer's accusation, in *History of the Church*, Vol. 6, pp. 354-355.

[45] *History of the Church*, Vol. 6, p. 411.

made that boast, "No man really knows my history."

Since Ms. Brodie came from the highest echelons of the church her book caused quite a stir. Great effort was given to discrediting it, but her work was thoroughly footnoted and documented. With her access to the church archives she brought out material not previously known.

Chapter twenty-four of her book is entitled, "The Wives of the Prophet." Brodie gives the names and ages of Joseph's wives. This list names 49 women, the youngest of which was 15 and oldest 59.

Joseph's wife Emma never seemed able to accept her husband's other wives. This was probably because she knew her husband better than anyone else did.

Fawn Brodie tells the following anecdote:

> Of the six wives who lived for long periods in the Mansion House, apparently only the thirty-nine-year-old poetess Eliza Snow conceived a child. She as well as Emma, it seems, was pregnant in the spring of 1844. Eliza must have been torn between dread of the consequences and exaltation at the prospect of facing the world the mother of a prophet's son.

> It happened that her bedroom in the Mansion House was to the left of Joseph's, Emma being on the right. According to tradition in the Snow family, Eliza emerged one morning at the same moment as Joseph, and he caught her to him in a quick embrace. At this instant Emma opened her own door and in a sudden terrible rage—for apparently she had trusted Eliza above all other women—seized a broomstick and began beating her. Eliza tried to flee, stumbled, and fell down the full flight of stairs. Still not content, Emma pursued her in a frenzy, that Joseph was powerless to stop, and drove her out of the house in her night dress. By this time the whole Mansion House was awake, young

Joseph and Alexander weeping and frightened at their mother's hysteria and begging her to be kind to the Aunt Eliza they adored.

Joseph finally calmed his wife and indignantly ordered her to restore Eliza to her room and rights in the household. The fall, it is said, resulted in a miscarriage. After Joseph's death Eliza married Brigham Young, but bore him no children.[46]

Polygamy was kept very quiet for many years because of its impact on public sentiment.

If polygamy was ordained by God as Joseph claimed, why then all the subterfuge, lying, and smoke screens? It was because the leaders of this movement were self-condemned men, living a lie. They were ashamed of their behavior, realized that it was wrong, and knew it would have devastating results on them. While they remained in the midwest, they continued to deny the practice of polygamy.

But when the Mormons moved to the vast reaches of Utah they were decidedly more bold in their practices. They felt secure now that they were farther away from the control of the United States government. It was only then that they openly advocated their practice of polygamy. When the Saints moved to Utah and practiced polygamy openly, the United States put pressure on them to desist.

It was at this time that information was published which documented the practice of polygamy by Joseph Smith and those who followed him. Church records

---

[46]Fawn Brodie, *No Man Knows My History*, pp. 345-346.

were made available that revealed the truth about Joseph Smith's sexual behavior and polygamy became public knowledge.

Heber C. Kimball, first counselor to Brigham Young, wrote:

> I speak of plurality of wives as one of the most holy principles that God ever revealed to man, and all those who exercise an influence against it, unto whom it is taught, man or woman, will be damned . . . the curse of God will be upon them . . . .[47]

Once again, honesty did not prove to be a high priority for the Mormon church leaders. The United States government made the Mormon church promise to stop its practice of polygamy. The church leaders promised to quit, but their promises were just empty words. The Mormons persisted in their practice (even until the present day).

As with all false doctrines, polygamy has brought inestimable suffering to Mormon women. There is a trail of tears associated with almost every case of polygamy.

Think of the hours of loneliness that these women must experience. Think of the potential for jealousy, unequal treatment and the feelings of rejection that must plague these relationships. Think of the competition for love and acceptance that must permeate this family structure. The end result of this system is not only seen in the weakening of the family unit (there is a great resentment between wives who think that the

---

[47] *Journal of Discourses*, Vol. 11, p. 211.

others are receiving more love and attention), but each individual involved suffers deep sorrow and bitterness. Polygamy is not only wrong; it violates basic human nature.

Joseph's wife, Emma, responded like most women would if they found their husband in a polygamous affair. When Emma learned that her husband had been intimate with another woman living in their home, she chased her down the stairs, out of the house and into the street while she was still in her night clothes.

It has also been reported that Brigham Young's wives would sometimes go a year without speaking a word to each other at the dinner table. Could this be why he called their home in Salt Lake City the "Lion House?"

The grief of the polygamist wife continues today. Polygamy (though not officially sanctioned by the L.D.S. church today) still continues. A 1967 magazine article was titled, "Twenty-five Thousand Polygamists in Utah." We believe that this figure was indeed accurate in 1967, but would also suggest that it is much larger today.

AN ENCOUNTER WITH POLYGAMY

We lived in Salt Lake City from 1966 until 1973. During these years I encountered many victims of polygamy. One afternoon, while I was in the church office, a man called and asked if I did marriage counseling. I replied that this service was available for members of the church. He reminded me that his wife was a member of our church and made an appointment to come in later that week.

As it turned out, this was the husband of a woman whom I had previously led out of the Mormon church. Although I had worked with this lady on several occasions, I had never had the opportunity to meet her husband. I hadn't given much thought to the particular circumstances until this phone call reminded me of an unusual event that had taken place several weeks before.

The lady, whom I will call Diane (not her real name), had been faithful in her attendance, but for some reason had not been present for about two weeks. Concerned for her well being, I had taken one of my associates with me to call on her.

When we arrived and knocked on the door, Diane answered, but would only talk while standing behind the door out of our view. She asked us not to worry about her and told us that she would be back to church soon. Diane assured us that she was all right, but had a good reason for being absent.

When Diane returned to church the following Sunday, she was wearing dark glasses that only partially covered the remainder of what had been a terribly black eye and a discolored nose. On most occasions, Diane was an extraordinarily beautiful woman with two children (a son and daughter), but on this particular day she was not so beautiful.

"Please do not ask what has happened to my face," she said.

I did not ask.

This phone call from her husband (whom I had never

met and who did not come to church), prompted me to wonder about this event—in my mind, I questioned whether he might have beaten her.

When they came to the office I visited with them both, and then he asked to speak with me privately. We talked for quite a while during which time he encouraged me to speak with his wife about subjection. He felt that subjection was the duty of a wife—especially a wife who claimed to be a Christian.

I asked specific questions as to how she was not being a good wife and he answered in a very vague and evasive way. He seemed to want to talk with me, but did not know how to begin.

After about twenty minutes I asked to speak with Diane. Trying to uncover the underlying events, I asked her to spell out the problem for me. She was also very vague and would not give me any specific information. She kept saying, "It is George that wanted to come see you, not me."

Finally I asked if George had struck her and given her the black eye. She responded affirmatively, but refused to tell me what was going on between them. I knew that there was a serious problem, but she insisted that I should ask George about it. After all, "it was his fault and not hers."

I then asked George to come back into my office and I talked with both of them together. Again, he was unwilling to tell me the nature of the problem.

Finally he blurted out, "If I tell you what is wrong, you will counsel divorce and I love Diane."

My reply was, "I never counsel divorce; it is not my place." He countered, "You would in this case!"

I was puzzled and asked, "Are you a polygamist?"

To which he replied, "Yes."

Then the whole story came out as a flood.

Diane said, "He wants me to give my consent for him to take another wife, but I love him and do not want to share him with any more women. The other woman is bad enough and this will make three of us."

The counseling session accomplished very little. George was adamant that he loved the new woman and he believed that it was his God given duty to take as many wives as he could—the *Doctrine and Covenants* demanded it.

I reminded him that the L.D.S. church no longer permitted the members to have more than one wife. To which he responded, "Yes, the church no longer follows the scriptures, but I do, as do many thousands of other L.D.S. people."

I know of several other prominent families that were "practicing the fundamentals of their faith." These people are known as "fundamentalists."

Diane's life became almost intolerable and after several more months of trying to reason with George, she decided to divorce him. Diane was left with two small children and two sister wives with half-brothers and half-sisters to her own children. In many respects her life was damaged beyond any hope of repair.

Diane told me of the lonely days when she was left isolated with the children while George was out courting the other wives. She told of how she often needed him, but he had commitments to other women or was off trying to win another woman's affection.

When George found a new flame, he would get all animated and go around in a cloud for days. These relationships usually didn't last long after the new girlfriend found out about his wives. She said that polygamy was a terrible dehumanizing thing that had left her devastated, with children, and many horrid memories.

False doctrine ruins people's lives. So much of what Joseph Smith has added to Christianity has been ruinous. Truth builds people and families up. Falsehood and lies always bear the seeds of death within them.

JOSEPH SMITH'S WIVES

But let's examine Joseph Smith's personal life a little more closely. Joseph Smith's sexual behavior is not one that would be expected from a godly man. Even if only a small part of what is recorded in history about him is true, he must have had as strong a sex drive as he did a physical drive.

Andrew Jensen, assistant L.D.S. church historian, listed 27 women who were married to Joseph.[48] The Mormon author John J. Steward credits him with even more, possibly three to four dozen or more.[49] Fawn M. Brodie, niece of church President David O. McKay, lists the names of 49 who were married to him. [50] In addition to these wives with whom Joseph Smith lived physically, there were 229 other living and 246 deceased women to which he was sealed for eternity.[51]

Some of the women who were sealed to Joseph Smith were married to other men after he died. One such

---

[48] *The Historical Record*, pp. 233,234.

[49] John Stewart, *Brigham Young and His Wives*, p. 31.

[50] Fawn Brodie, *No Man Knows my History*, pp. 434-465 lists 48 wives besides Emma; pp. 335-336 lists 49 wives including Emma.

[51] *Ibid*.

woman was the wife of Heber C. Kimball. Even though she had nine children by Heber, he would have to surrender her in the resurrection to Joseph, according to L.D.S. church doctrine.

According to the history done by Fawn Brodie, Joseph's youngest wife was only 15 when he consummated the relationship with her, and her sister was only 16 when he first violated her. Would it not be fair to say that he was a dirty old man?

Why doesn't the women's liberation movement today speak up when the church still teaches that exaltation can be only achieved by those men who have more than one wife sealed to them for eternity?

For a Mormon woman, heaven is one long pregnancy as she helps her husband people his heaven.

Mormon doctrine teaches that a Mormon man is to call his wife or wives from the grave in the resurrection.

CHAPTER NINE

The Fighter

A fourth reason for the Mormons to be ashamed of Joseph Smith is because the Bible teaches that a church leader is not to be "a brawler."[52]

Joseph Smith loved to fight and then brag about his physical powers. It is true that he was an extraordinarily strong person physically.

> John D. Lee related that one day Joseph Smith and some of his men were wrestling. Because it was "the Sabbath day" Sidney Rigdon tried to break it up. Joseph Smith "dragged him from the ring, bareheaded, and tore Rigdon's fine pulpit coat from the collar to the waist; then he turned to the men and said: Go in, boys, and have your fun."[53]

---

[52] 1 Timothy 3:3
[53] *Confessions of John D. Lee*, pp. 76-78.

Calvin Stoddard once testified that:

> Smith then came up and knocked him in the forehead
> with his flat hand—the blow knocked him down, when
> Smith repeated the blow four or five times, very hard—
> it made him blind—that Smith afterwards came to him
> and asked his forgiveness . . . .[54]

In Joseph Smith's diary under January 1-2, 1843,
Joseph Smith related that he had "whipped" seven men
at once and on another occasion had "whipped" a Baptist minister "till he begged."

With these things in mind, how does the Mormon
prophet fare when compared to Jesus Christ? After all,
the Mormon church has claimed "no better man ever
lived than Joseph Smith."

The Book of Isaiah records the temperament of Jesus:

> He was despised and forsaken of men, a man of sor-
> rows, and acquainted with grief; and like one from
> whom men hide their face, He was despised, and we
> did not esteem Him. Surely our griefs He Himself bore,
> and our sorrows He carried; Yet we ourselves esteemed
> Him stricken, smitten of God, and afflicted. But *He was
> pierced through for our transgressions, He was crushed for
> our iniquities; the chastening for our well being fell upon
> Him, and by His scourging we are healed.* All of us like
> sheep have gone astray, each of us has turned to his own
> way; But the Lord has caused the iniquity of us all to fall
> on Him. *He was oppressed and He was afflicted, Yet He did
> not open His mouth; Like a lamb that is led to slaughter, and
> like a sheep that is silent before its shearers, So He did not
> open His mouth.* By oppression and judgment He was
> taken away; And as for His generation, who considered
> that He was cut off out of the land of the living, for the

---

[54] Max Parkin, *Conflict at Kirtland*, p. 132.

transgression of my people to whom the stroke was due? His grave was assigned with wicked men, yet He was with a rich man in death, *Because He had done no violence, nor was there any deceit in His mouth.*[55]

When Jesus spoke of Himself He said:

Come to Me, all who are weary and heavy-laden, and I will give you rest. Take My yoke upon you, and learn from Me, for I am gentle and humble in heart; and you shall find rest for your souls. For My yoke is easy, and My load is light.

Was Jesus a brawler? How about Stephen? Paul? Peter?

It is true that at the betrayal of Christ in the Garden of Gethsemane, a disciple took a sword and cut off the ear of a high priest's servant, but Jesus said that the act of violence was not appropriate and He healed one of the very men who had come to take Him into custody.[56] Jesus told His disciple:

Put your sword back into its place; for all those who take up the sword shall perish by the sword. Or do you think that I cannot appeal to My Father, and He will at once put at My disposal more than twelve legions of angels?[57]

Jesus could have acted in a very prolific way. But He didn't! I wonder what Jesus would think of Joseph Smith's theatrics? No wonder the Mormons are "ashamed of Joseph."

---

[55] Isaiah 53:3-9, NASB. Italics mine.
[56] Luke 22:51
[57] Matthew 26:52, 53

CHAPTER TEN

The Commanding Officer

We have already seen that Jesus commanded His servants not to fight. Jesus Himself could have called legions of angels to help Him—but He didn't.

How does Joseph Smith compare? Only four years after Joseph Smith published the *Book of Mormon* he organized an army to march to "Missouri to redeem Zion." During his short lifetime he had more than one militia. This is only one example of such a band. Joseph also had a group called "The Danites," and another called "The Avenging Angels."

Many efforts have been expended by Mormon authorities to exonerate Joseph Smith in regard to the

Danites, but these efforts have proven fruitless.

It is, therefore, necessary to this discussion to show that Joseph Smith was responsible for the group called the Danites. Because of the damaging nature of this charge, the Latter-day Saints have made a valiant effort to disprove that he ever had anything to do with them. Again they are shown to be dishonest in presenting the real truth.

The Mormon writer William E. Berrett admits that,

> Such a band as the Danites did exist, as historians affirm . . . The organization had been for the purpose of plundering and murdering the enemies of the Saints.[58]

Although he documents the existence of such a band of people he tries to disprove that the church leaders were responsible for their existence.

But David Whitmer, one of the three witnesses to the *Book of Mormon*, says:

> . . . They issued a decree organizing what was termed the "Danites, or Destroying Angels," who were bound by the most fearful oaths to obey the commandment of the leaders of the church. The Danites consisted only of those selected by Smith and Rigdon. They t(h)reatened myself, John Whitmer, Oliver Cowdery and Lyman Johnson with the vengeance of the Danites . . . .[59]

Evidence proves that Joseph Smith was responsible for this group of cutthroats. Certainly the church is ashamed of his part in it and would want to deny it. They should be ashamed.

Thomas B. Marsh, who had been President of the

---

[58]William E. Berrett, *The Restored Church*, pp. 197-198.

[59] *Kansas City Daily Journal*, June 5, 1881.

Council of the Twelve Apostles, made this statement in a sworn affidavit on October 24, 1838:

> They have among them a company, considered true Mormons, called the Danites, who have taken an oath to support the heads of the Church in all things that they say or do, whether right or wrong. Many, however, of this band are much dissatisfied with this oath, as being against moral and religious principles.[60]

Most of what Joseph Smith did was not original with him, but borrowed from some other source. The idea for the Danites may have come from Joseph's Masonry. A part of Masonry is a pledge of mutual defense in times of crisis. Joseph took this idea way beyond what was ever dreamed of in the Masonic Lodge.

Another evidence for the early origin of the Danites is found in the *Diary of Hosea Stout*.

> We then had a drill muster for an (h)our or so. I took the command by order of the Col. After drilling a while I took them through the old Missouri Danite drill.[61]

Oliver Cowdery blames Sidney Rigdon for influencing Joseph Smith to begin the Danites.

> I never dreamed, however, that he (Sidney Rigdon) would influence the Prophet, Seer, and Revelator to the Church of the Latter Day Saints, into the formation of a secret band at Far West, committed to depredations upon Gentiles and the actual assassination of apostates from the church, which was done in June last, and was only one of many wrong steps.[62]

---

[60] *History of the Church*, Vol. 3, p. 167, footnote.

[61] *On the Mormon Frontier, The Diary of Hosea Stout*, Vol. 1, p. 197.

[62] Oliver Cowdery, *Defense*, p. 2, as quoted by Jerald and Sandra Tanner, *Mormonism, Shadow or Reality?*, p. 347.

Former Mormon church president Joseph Fielding Smith confirmed the existence of the Danites.

Thomas B. Marsh, President of the council of the Twelve Apostles, suddenly left Far West in October, 1838 . . . Orson Hyde, in the same spirit, followed him on the 18th of October. On the 24th, Marsh went before Henry Jacobs, justice of the peace at Richmond, and made an affidavit the gist of which is as follows:

They have among them a company considered true "Mormons," called the Danites, who have taken an oath to support the heads of the Church in all things that they say or do, whether right or wrong. Many, however, of this band are much dissatisfied with this oath, as being against moral and religious principles. On Saturday last, I am informed by the "Mormons," that they had a meeting at Far West at which they appointed a company of twelve, by the name of the "Destruction Company," for the purpose of burning and destroying . . . I have heard the prophet say that he would yet tread down his enemies, and walk over their dead bodies; and if he was not let alone, he would be a second Mohammed to this generation, and that he would make it one gore of blood from the Rocky Mountains to the Atlantic Ocean; that like Mohammed, whose motto in treating for peace was, "the Alcoran (Koran) or the Sword" so should it be eventually with us, "Joseph Smith or the Sword." These last statements were made during the last summer. The number of armed men at Adam-ondi-Ahman was between three and four hundred.

Thomas B. Marsh.

Sworn to and Subscribed before me, the day herein written.
Henry Jacobs, J.P.,
Ray County, Missouri.

Richmond, Missouri, October 24, 1838.

Affidavit of Orson Hyde

The most of the statements in the forgoing disclosure I
know to be true; the remainder I believe to be true.

Orson Hyde
Richmond, Missouri, October 24, 1838.

Sworn to and subscribed before me, on the day written.
Henry Jacobs, J.P.[63]

All efforts to disprove Joseph Smith's involvement in
the society of the Danites is only a documentation of
our basic thesis that the Mormon church is truly
ashamed of Joseph Smith's actions.

History does give us a clear picture of the work of the
Danites. The successor to Joseph Smith in the Utah
Branch church was Brigham Young. One of the saddest
pages of the history of the settling of the West is the part
played by the Danites and Utah Militia.

These groups could well have been the ones who led
the Mountain Meadow Massacre and many other
evils.[64]

Let us take up the history of the grisly work done by
this group under the direction of Joseph's successor,
Brigham Young. Ask yourself the question, "Why were
the Mormons always being run out of places?" The
answer may well be found in part in this part of their
history.

---

[63] Joseph Fielding Smith, *Essentials in Church History*, pp.
225-227.

[64] See *The Mountain Meadow Massacre, or The Life and Confessions of John D. Lee.*

Brigham Young still had the Danites after the Mormons came to Utah.

> If men come here and do not behave themselves, they will not only find the Danites, whom they talk so much about, biting the horses' heels, but the scoundrels will find them biting their heels. In my plain remarks, I merely call things by their right names. Brother Kimball is noted in the States for calling things by their right names, and you will excuse me if I do the same.[65]

It isn't surprising that the Latter-day Saints are ashamed of this group of cutthroats. They should be ashamed of Joseph Smith's part in it all.

The Danites killed many people, terrorized others, and in general acted as Joseph's bodyguards. They struck fear into the hearts of people.

A MORMON ASSASSIN

Later Brigham Young had a bodyguard named Bill Hickman who killed people upon his orders. Bill's history is recounted in a book entitled *Bill Hickman's Confession* or *Brigham's Destroying Angel*.

This book's subtitle is "Bill Hickman, The Danite Chief of Utah." The book was published in 1904. Hickman had a long history of violence that began when he was 12 or 13. Here is a brief account in his own words.

> About the time I was twelve or thirteen year old, I performed my first feat of bravery. My father had several hundred head of hogs which roamed the woods, and needed no feed except when the ground was frozen; then they

---

[65] *Journal of Discourses*, Vol. 5, p. 6.

would gather in, and with them wild ones, having tremendous teeth sticking out of their mouths, and they would attack persons frequently. My father sent me to the mill to feed the hogs out of the toll corn in the mill, at the same time telling me to look out for the wild boars. I finished and started to the house, which was three or four hundred yards and had gone about half-way, when I looked behind me and saw a huge wild boar coming full tilt after me, not more than fifty steps behind. I started homeward for life, and an old hunting dog met me at the top of his speed, almost knocking me down as he passed. After making a few jumps, I stopped and turned to see the fight; I saw a fearful gash in the dog's shoulder, but he had the boar by the ear, and that moment fear turned into anger, and saying to myself, "I will kill you or die in the attempt," I picked up what we then called a hand-spike, which lay by the roadside, and made for the hog. But I had to back three or four times, as he would run at me with the dog holding to him. After a while I got a blow across his back, which brought his hind parts to the ground. I followed up my blows, the old dog holding to him, notwithstanding he had received three severe wounds, one on his neck, which I thought would be fatal from the flowing of the blood. But, faithful to his young master, whenever I would shout, 'Hold him tight, Catch,' he would go in while I struck the boar on the back and loins. I then took out my pocket-knife and cut his ham-strings, then cut a hole in his side, and literally gutted him, a handful at a time. I saw him dying, and for the first time, after speaking to the dog, he let him go.

I went home all bloody, went in and met father; he looked at me and asked what was the matter. I told him. He turned pale, then said I must be mistaken. He shouldered his gun and went with me. The first thing I showed him was the dog; poor fellow, he had stopped bleeding and lay stretched in the door-yard. Father said he had never seen such teeth before. He gave me orders not to go out any more until the hogs had all gone for the woods again . . . .[66]

---

[66] Bill Hickman, *Brigham's Destroying Angel*, pp. 29-30.

When Bill was about 14 or 15 he killed a panther.

"Bill, take the gun, and go and see what those dogs have treed." I started with a gun and a knife, went about half a mile, and saw in a tree a large, full-grown panther, and the dogs under the tree. The hair stood straight upon my head; but I roused my courage, cocked my gun, and approached within fifty yards of the tree, when the savage-looking monster spied me. He leaped from the tree, and the dogs, six in number, four blood-hounds and two strong curs, caught him. I ran up, but there was such a turning and rolling that I feared to shoot, seeing no chance to do so without hitting some of the dogs. I drew my knife, as I saw him stretched by the dogs, and made a lunge for him; but he saw me, and made another effort, breaking loose from the cur that had him by the neck, and reached his paw for me, making a heavy stroke. He caught my pants just below the waist-band, and took out a strip about three inches wide, clear to the bottom. I turned and saw the dogs had covered him almost, but he was getting up, some having hold one place and some another. All his legs were held by the dogs but one. I made a sudden break, and stabbed him through the heart the first blow, jumped back, and shouted to the dogs. I saw him weaken, and soon he was dead. He was too heavy for me to carry; it was all I wanted to do to lift him. I went home and told the news, but was not believed until we went and packed the huge animal in. My pants I had tied up with hickory bark until I got home. The story about the strip torn out of them was too big to be believed, and they said it was not so—that I had torn them on a snag, or running through the brush; but when we went to get him the strip was in his claws, and stuck fast, and that was the evidence beyond doubt that I had run a great risk . . . .[67]

Later Bill Hickman was just as quick to carry out the orders of Brigham Young to "ride someone over the

---

[67] *Ibid.*, pp. 31-32.

edge of the canyon, or waste them." Bill Hickman had a very colorful life, but the previous stories pale in comparison to the stories he tells about the time in which he served Brigham Young as a Danite.

While serving in the Utah Militia Bill says:

We went down to see the Indians we had shot. Hirons told me I had killed the chief, Big Elk. I took off his head, for I had heard the old mountaineer, Jim Bridger, say he would give a hundred dollars for it. I tied it in his blanket and laid it on a flat rock; hid his gun and bow and arrows, forty-two in number one good arrows, and awaited the arrival of the company . . . The companies soon came up, when we attacked and killed nearly all the Indians. We took about fifty women and children prisoners. When I came to where I had killed the chief, I had to laugh. Those rear fellows who had been in the habit of picking up everything, had untied the blanket that was around the chief's head, but on seeing what it contained left it untied with the head sitting in the middle of it, entirely untouched. I took the head, gun, bow and arrows, mounted my horse, took a pretty squaw behind me and a sick papoose in front, and was off for our quarters.[68]

In another battle in the Utah Indian Wars Bill says:

We got within gun shot of the Indians before they saw us. The boys made a rush on them, shooting, hooting, and yelling in such a manner that they all took fright before firing a gun or shooting an arrow. The boys dashed into the brush, keeping up a constant firing, and the Indians rose around us as thick almost as a gang of sheep. I never saw the like. They took down the river into large and thick brush. I saw up the hill, about a mile

---

[68] *Ibid.*, p. 68.

off, one of my men after an Indian. He shot at him, wheeled his horse, and started back. I had just emptied one slide of my gun, six loads, and had no other slide with me. One of my men had a good rifle, which I took and started at full speed over the sage brush, met the man and asked him what was the matter. He said he had shot off his gun and both pistols, and had no more ammunition with him. In about two miles I overtook the Indian. He had got close to the mountain, and had two arrows left, which he turned loose at me. One of them cut my coat collar. I saw he had no more, rode within a rod of him, and busted a cap at him. I then made a drive for him on my horse. He was the largest Indian I ever saw, and ran like a scared wolf. I caught my gun by the breech, ran on him and struck him over the head with such a force I broke the gun off at the breech. The barrel fell some ten feet off, and the Indian in front of me, and my horse fell over him. I lit on my feet, jumped and caught up the gun-barrel, and wheeled for the Indian. He was getting up when I hit him again over the head, killing him instantly, the blow bending the heavy barrel four inches. I jerked off his scalp and went back as fast as my horse could carry me.

On the bluff of the river sat Doc. Ripley on his horse, over an Indian he said he had killed. Said he to me: "Captain, take off his scalp for me, as your hands are bloody. I am not spleeny about such things. I have cut up many a dead person in the dissecting rooms." I dismounted, caught him by the top of his head, and as soon as I began to cut, he jumped straight on his feet. I stabbed him with my knife a few times, which soon ended him . . . .[69]

Brigham's Danite Chief was a bloodthirsty old militia man.

On another occasion Bill Hickman was asked to terminate Richard Yates. Yates was a trader who was sus-

---

[69] *Ibid.*, pp. 74-75.

pected of supplying government troops with ammunition. Let's take up the story:

> We traveled about fifty miles and camped on Yellow
> Creek. The next morning we traveled about half-way
> down Echo Canon to where the general's headquarters
> were located, and got breakfast. I delivered General
> Wells some letters, reported myself, and told him who I
> had along, and asked him what I should do with my
> prisoner. He said: "He ought to be killed; but take him
> on; you will probably get an order when you get to Col.
> Jones' camp" —which was at the mouth of Echo Canon
> on Weber River. After breakfast we started for Jones'
> camp, some twelve miles distant, and when within three
> or four miles of the camp, we met Joseph A. Young, a
> son of Brigham's going, as he said, to the general's camp
> to take orders. He hailed me (I being behind) and said
> his father wanted that man Yates killed, and that I
> would know all about it when I go to Jones' camp.
>
> We got there about sundown and were met outside by
> Col. Jones, and conducted around under the hill, below
> and just outside of his camp . . . He then took me aside
> and told me he had orders when Yates came along to
> have him used up, and that was why he had taken me
> outside of his camp . . . I remained at our camp-fire until
> eleven or twelve o'clock that night, several coming and
> chatting with me.
>
> About the time all was still, and everybody supposed to
> be in their beds. No person was to be seen, when Col.
> Jones and two others, Hosea Stout and another man
> whose name I do not recollect, came to my camp-fire
> and asked if Yates was asleep. I told them he was, upon
> which his brains were knocked out with an ax . . . .[70]

They dug a grave, buried him and moved their fire

---

[70] *Ibid.*, pp. 124-125.

over the new grave to hide its location from others who might come along. Bill took Yates's belongings and gave them to Brigham. In his own words;

> The next day I took the nine hundred dollars, and we all went to headquarters (In Salt Lake City). Flack and I had a talk, as we went, about the money. He said Brigham ought to give that to us as we had already been to more expense than that money amounted to, from horses used up and other losses, and urged me to get it . . . .

> Soon after dark Flack and I went to Brigham's office. He asked how things were going on out East, and I told him. He asked what had become of Yates? I told him. He then asked if I had got word from him? I told him that I had got his instructions at Jones' camp, and also of the word I had from his son Jo. He said that was right, and a good thing. I then told him I had nine hundred dollars given me to bring in, that Yates had at the time he was captured. I told him of the expense I had been to during the war, and asked him if I might have part of the money? He gave me a reprimand for asking such a thing, and said it must go towards defraying the expenses of the war . . . I pulled out the sack . . . The money was counted, and we left.[71]

The battle was between U.S. Troops and the Mormon Militia. Can you imagine killing a man whose crime was supplying powder to the U.S. Troops?

Yates was robbed, placed in leg irons, then when fast asleep killed by Hickman with an ax. It is a bloodthirsty and disgusting account that shows the fruits borne by the Danites, begun and commissioned by Joseph Smith.

---

[71] *Ibid.*, pp. 126-127.

Finally the break came with Bill Hickman and Brigham Young. Brigham did not know his true feeling towards him so he asked Bill to first kidnap General Connor of the United States. For this service he offered him one thousand dollars. Later he wanted him to kill him and offered him far more. Let us hear it in Bill Hickman's own words:

> And here I will state that just before this I had my last break with Brigham Young. In the spring or early summer of 1863 I went in town, and Brigham Young sent for me. When I got to his place he said: "That Gen. Connor is nothing but an Irish ditcher, and don't belong in this country, and you are the man to get him out of it." After some more talk he said, "If I would kidnap Connor and set him over into California, he would attend to the help and give me one thousand dollars, and all expenses paid." I laughed at this, and made no reply. Nobody knew then how I stood, and I did not know how they looked on me. Six months after that Brigham Young repeated his previous conversation with me, and said Connor was a bad man, calculated to do a great deal of injury to this people, and ought to be used up. Now, said he, you are the man to do it; you travel with him as pilot and guide, and it could be laid to the Indians. You can have a great deal more money than if you had kidnapped him and taken him to California.[72]

At that point Bill Hickman had hard words with Brigham Young and it was the beginning of his end. Bill later went to jail because of his crimes—but it was many years later. While the Mormon church had jurisdiction in Utah, no action was taken against him though he was made the scapegoat for many crimes committed by the

---

[72] *Ibid.*, pp. 166-167.

church. The Mormons protected Hickman because they did not want him to open his mouth to tell what he knew.

Often Bill was referred to as a murderer and an evil man, but it was not until the United States government took action that he was brought to trial and subsequently Brigham Young was also arrested.

The purpose of this lengthy narrative is to follow the growth of the seeds planted by Joseph Smith to their full harvest. From the very beginning, Joseph resisted authority, used intimidation tactics, physical force, whippings and beatings, to silence those who spoke against him. First there had been "The Whittlers," then "The Avenging Angels," and finally "The Danites."

As the United States grew, it was no longer possible to get away with such practices. This chapter of the life of Joseph Smith is one in which Mormons are justifiably ashamed.

No doubt about it, Joseph was a brave man—but he was certainly a false prophet and has established a false religion.

CHAPTER ELEVEN

King on Earth

In carrying out our comparison of Joseph Smith and Jesus, it would serve us well to remember what Jesus said about power, authority, and the establishment of an earthly kingdom. By the first century, people had long been expecting the Messiah to come and establish an earthly rule. If Jesus had wanted to establish an earthly kingdom, he could have done so with great success. Jesus had not only the ability, but the opportunity to establish such a kingdom.

Do you remember the account of the temptations of Jesus? Satan offered to put Jesus in charge of all the kingdoms of the world and to give Him all the glory that He deserved. But Jesus told Satan to "begone."[73]

---

[73] Matthew 4:8-10

Jesus was not after earthly power. He did not want to be an earthly king. Jesus was not out to serve Himself, or even continue to grasp equality with God,

> but emptied Himself, taking the form of a bond-servant, and being made in the likeness of men. And being found in appearance as a man, He humbled Himself by becoming obedient to the point of death, even death on a cross.[74]

At another point in His life, His disciples came forward and asked to be given a position of authority in His earthly kingdom. Remember what Jesus had to say to them:

> You know that the rulers of the Gentiles lord it over them, and their great men exercise authority over them. It is not so among you, but whoever wishes to become great among you shall be your servant, and whoever wishes to be first among you shall be your slave; just as the Son of Man did not come to be served, but to serve, and give His life a ransom for many.[75]

Jesus was not out to glorify Himself, but to glorify His Father in heaven.

Can the same be said about Joseph Smith? Did you know that before Joseph Smith died he had himself ordained king? This is a fact that few people realize. It is evident that toward the end of his life, Joseph became obsessed with a desire for power and authority. This is another aspect of the life of Joseph Smith that Mormon leaders have tried to deny or repress. Some historians

---

[74] Philippians 2:6-8
[75] Matthew 20:25-28

have even tried to dismiss such claims as speculation and rumor. These claims when researched, however, are substantiated.

> Rumors implying that the Prophet assumed royal pretensions are somewhat substantiated by George Miller who stated on one occasion that "In this council we ordained Joseph Smith as King on earth."[76]

Joseph Smith also ran for the office of President of the United States in 1844. Smith wanted to place the government under his rule and under the authority of the Mormon church. Orson Hyde said,

> What the world calls "Mormonism" will rule every nation. Joseph Smith and Brigham Young will be the head. God has decreed it, and his own right arm will accomplish it.[77]

On January 29, 1844 in the *History of the Church*, Joseph Smith is quoted as saying,

> . . . to accomplish this, you must send every man in the city who is able to speak in public throughout the land to electioneer. . . . There is oratory enough in the Church to carry me into the presidential chair . . . .[78]

Joseph wanted power and authority. He wanted to establish an earthly kingdom where he could be king. His desire was to sit at the head of the table and draw

---

[76] Klaus J. Hansen, "The Theory and Practice of the Political Kingdom of God in Mormon History, 1829-1890, " master's thesis, BYU, 1959, typed copy, p. 114.

[77] *Journal of Discourses*, 7:53.

[78] *History of the Church*, Vol. 6, p. 243.

attention to himself. Joseph wanted to wear a crown on his head and proclaim himself "King on Earth." He coveted the presidency for the same reasons.

Jesus wore a crown on His head—it was the crown of thorns that was placed there by the Roman soldiers. Jesus was proclaimed King, but it was not a title that He chose for Himself. "King of the Jews" was a name that was given to Him while He was on the cross. It was His crucifiers who hung the sign in an attempt to mock Him.[79]

There is another comparison we might make between Jesus Christ and Joseph Smith. Joseph died in prison at a young age at the hands of his enemies. Jesus also died. He too was very young. Jesus died the death of a criminal at the hand of his accusers. The difference? Joseph died in a gunfight, killing two men and wounding another.[80] Jesus died, forgiving his enemies because they didn't know what they were doing, saving a thief on the cross, and delivering mankind from the bondage of sin.

Is there any wonder why Christians worldwide give their admiration and devotion to their leader and Savior? Is there any wonder why the Mormon church is ashamed of their leader?

When a person carefully examines the character of Joseph Smith, there is little doubt as to why the Mormon church is "ashamed of Joseph."

---

[79] Mark 15:16-26

[80] Loyal Mormons refer to Joseph as being a martyr. History tells us, however, that a martyr is a person who willingly submits his life to his enemies and peacefully awaits the ultimate justice of God.

ASHAMED OF HIS ROLE AS A PROPHET

*Also it will come about
in that day
that the prophets
will each be ashamed
of his vision
when he prophesies . . . .*

Zechariah 13:4

CHAPTER TWELVE

The Prophet

When a prophet speaks in the name of the Lord, if the thing does not come about or come true, that is the thing which the Lord has not spoken. The prophet has spoken it presumptuously; you shall not be afraid of him.[81]

Down through the centuries God has chosen to communicate His message through men. The book of Hebrews tells us that God spoke through the prophets "in many portions and in many ways" and has most recently spoken through His Son.[82] The New Testament also warns us that many people will come after Christ who claim to speak on behalf of God, and commands us

---

[81] Deuteronomy 18:22
[82] Hebrews 1:1, 2

to test them to see if they measure up to biblical guide-lines.[83] Fortunately for us, the Bible gives us some clear-cut principles by which we can determine whether a prophet is truly from God or whether he is a false prophet.

Deuteronomy 18:20-22 (quoted at the beginning of this chapter) contains one of these tests. From this text we know that when true prophets spoke—they spoke on behalf of God. Since God cannot lie or be mistaken (at least not the God of true Christianity), He required His prophets to be totally accurate when they spoke on His behalf. To be errant or misguided in a prophecy was a sure sign that the prophet was not from God.[84] One false prophecy, one untrue word, one erroneous utterance on the part of the prophet and he would forever be disqualified as a true prophet of God.

In addition, even if a person claimed to be a prophet of God—even if he genuinely foretold future events, he was still to be rejected if he taught something that was in contradiction with what was known to be God's word.

And what was to be done with those who didn't measure up to biblical standards? In biblical times, a false prophet was to be put to death for claiming that he spoke on behalf of the Almighty.

Joseph Smith, Brigham Young, the Mormon presidents, and others within the Mormon church have

---

[83] See 2 Peter 2:1-3; 1 John 4:1-3; 2 Corinthians 11:13-15; Matthew 24:11, 24.

[84] See Deuteronomy 13:1-5; Isaiah 9:13-16; Jeremiah 14:13-16; Ezekiel 13:1-9.

claimed that they were prophets of God and able to speak on His behalf. One of the favorite titles for Joseph Smith is that of "Prophet." Even the current president refers to Joseph in this way:

> Joseph Smith was a prophet of the Living God, one of the greatest prophets that has ever lived upon the earth. . . . we have standing at the head of the Church today a prophet . . . who holds all the keys and authority necessary to carry forward our Father's program for the blessing of His children. . . . The greatest activity in this world or in the world to come is directly related to the work and mission of Joseph Smith—man of destiny, prophet of God.[85]

Mormons must admit that the legitimacy of their church rests on the basis that Joseph Smith was a "true" prophet of God. Joseph Smith himself claimed that the church began with his divine call. Mormon scriptures depend entirely upon Smith's prophetic utterances and are written accounts of the "messages" he received. Wouldn't it be interesting to see how Joseph measured up to biblical guidelines?

Let me list but a few of the over fifty prophetic utterances of Joseph Smith. Of all his predictions, it should be noted that only parts of two ever came to pass.[86] This means that Joseph Smith was very wrong. He was wrong almost 100% of the time.

---

[85] Ezra Taft Benson, *The Teachings of Ezra Taft Benson*, p. 104.

[86] In one of these predictions, Joseph supposedly predicted the Civil War. It is discussed later in this chapter. The second prophecy has come under scrutiny also. This might have been a prophecy recorded after the fact. For further details see Jerald and Sandra Tanner's book, *The Changing World of Mormonism*, page 404.

THE TEMPLE PROPHECY

Joseph Smith prophesied that a Mormon temple was to be built in Jackson County, Missouri before the generation living in 1832 passed away.

> A revelation of Jesus Christ unto his servant Joseph Smith, Jun., . . . Yea, the word of the Lord concerning his church, established in the last days for the restoration of his people, as he has spoken by the mouth of his prophets, and for the gathering of his saints to stand upon Mount Zion, which shall be the city of New Jerusalem. Which city shall be built, beginning at the temple lot, which is appointed by the finger of the Lord, in the western boundaries of the State of Missouri, and dedicated by the hand of Joseph Smith, Jun., and others with whom the Lord was well pleased. Verily this is the word of the Lord, that the city New Jerusalem shall be built by the gathering of the saints, beginning at this place, even the place of the temple, which temple shall be reared in this generation. For verily this generation shall not all pass away until an house shall be built unto the Lord, and a cloud shall rest upon it, which cloud shall be even the glory of the Lord which shall fill the house.[87]

This prophecy clearly teaches that a temple would be built in western Missouri in the generation of the men then living and that it would be dedicated by the hand of Joseph Smith himself. The apostles of the Mormon church were well aware of Smith's prophecy and declared many times that it would be fulfilled during the lifetime of those in existence in 1832.[88] Orson Pratt,

---

[87] *Doctrine and Covenants*, 84:1-5.
[88] *The Journal of Discourses*, Vol. 9, p. 71; Vol. 10, p. 344; Vol. 13, p. 362.

an apostle of the Mormon church, was still confident in 1870 that this prophecy would be fulfilled.

> The Latter-day Saints just as much expect to receive a fulfillment of that promise . . . as they expect that the sun will rise and set tomorrow. Why? Because God cannot lie. He will fulfill all His promises.[89]

Even ninety-nine years after Joseph's prophecy was given, the tenth president and prophet of the Mormon church believed that the temple and city would be built.

> Some of that generation who were living when this revelation was given. . . . I have full confidence in the word of the Lord that it shall not fail . . . . We have not been released from this responsibility, nor shall we be. The word of the Lord will not fail. . . . the city of Zion, or New Jerusalem, will eventually be built in Jackson County, Missouri and the temple of the Lord will also be constructed.[90]

I have in my possession the full transcripts of the court records of three Mormon branches of the L.D.S. church and their efforts to gain possession of this temple lot. The three groups consist of the Utah Branch, the Reorganized Branch, and the Hedrickites. To date, the Hedrickites have won the court battle.[91]

Needless to say, the city was not built; the temple was not constructed—Joseph's prophecy was false. The fact is, this single passage from the *Doctrine and Covenants* contains at least six false elements. In the 160 years

---

[89] Orson Pratt, *Journal of Discourses*, Vol. 9, p. 71.

[90] Joseph Fielding Smith, *Way to Perfection*, pp. 268-270.

[91] I would include the document in this book, but it is literally hundreds of pages long and would itself make a very large book.

following this prediction, 1) no temple has ever been built in western Missouri; 2) a Mormon city has not been established; 3) Joseph never dedicated the temple; 4) no sacrifices can ever be made; and 5) a cloud cannot rest on a nonexistent temple; and 6) even if it were yet to be constructed, the temple was not built in the generation of people then living.

In a feeble attempt to substantiate this prophecy, some Mormons suggest that Zion was "reestablished" in Salt Lake City and is a fulfillment of the prophecy. But the 1832 prophecy clearly states that there will be "none other place" than the western boundaries of Missouri, and Joseph Smith never made it to Salt Lake.

How does a faithful Mormon explain this? Mormons have devised various ways to "explain" false prophecies. They often claim, as Smith himself did, that a prophet is only a prophet when he is acting as such— that is, when he claims to speak in the name of the Lord and is under divine inspiration. Mormons claim that "errors" were made only when Smith was not acting as a "prophet."

But this explanation is not only unbiblical, it doesn't even help their case. Look back to the temple prophecy. It claims to be "A revelation of Jesus Christ . . ." Joseph clearly states that he was acting as a prophet, and that the message was from Jesus. There can be no doubt according to biblical standards that Joseph Smith was a false prophet. Even by Joseph's own standards he failed to measure up. Joseph Smith himself emphasized that a true prophet must have his prophecies evaluated by the standards of God's Word.

> The only way of ascertaining a true prophet is to compare his prophecies with the ancient Word of God, and see if they agree, and if they do and come to pass, then

106

certainly he is a true prophet. . . . When, therefore any man, no matter who, or how high his standing may be, utters, or publishes, anything that afterwards proves to be untrue, he is a false prophet.[92]

By Joseph's own words he is proven to be a false prophet, and by the very words of Mormon authorities the Mormon religion also falls.

Here are a few more examples of false prophecies of Joseph.

THE MISSOURI SETTLEMENT

Joseph Smith spoke often about the Mormon settlement in Jackson County, Missouri which he called Zion.

And the nations of the earth shall honor her, and shall say: Surely Zion is the city of our God, and surely Zion cannot fall, neither be moved out of her place, for God is there, and the hand of the Lord is there.[93]

Smith claimed that Zion could not fall or be moved out of her place. But two weeks before he made this prophecy, on July 20, 1833, Zion was moved! Officials of the Mormon church were tarred and feathered and literally run out of town. It is unfortunate that Smith was in Kirtland, Ohio at the time of this incident and was unaware of the problem in Missouri.[94] This supposed prophecy was wrong at the very instant it was given.

---

[92] *The Evening and Morning Star*, July 1833, p. 1.
[93] *Doctrine and Covenants*, 97:19.
[94] *Doctrine and Covenants*, 97:19. Given August 2, 1833.

THE RETURN OF CHRIST

Smith was also errant about the return of Christ. He promised in 1835[95] and again in 1843 that Christ would return around the year 1891. If you could read the original *History* (it has since been altered) taken from Smith's diary under the date, April 6, 1843 you would find the following:

> I prophecy [sic] in the name of the Lord God —& let it be written: that the Son of Man will not come in the heavens until I am 85 years old, 48 years hence or about 1890.[96]

Unfortunately, Joseph died a year later—and Christ still has not returned. At least this time Joseph was smart enough to put the date of fulfillment beyond that of his own lifetime!

THE MOON IS POPULATED

Joseph fabricated a story that the moon was populated by people who dressed like Quakers, were uniformly six feet tall, and lived to be 1000 years old.[97] Joseph Smith probably never imagined that men like Neil Armstrong would one day walk on the moon. Once again, Joseph is proven wrong!

---

[95] *History of the Church*, Vol. 2, p. 182.

[96] Cited from Jerald and Sandra Tanner, *The Changing World of Mormonism*, p. 419.

[97] Oliver B. Huntington, a follower of Joseph Smith, provides us with this information in Vol. 11, p. 166 of his *Journal*.

THE KIRTLAND NATIONAL BANK

Many people are unaware of Joseph Smith's banking establishment, much less his false predictions concerning this bank. Around 1837, the Kirtland Safety Society was started to provide a place for Mormons to "hold their treasures; and to aid them to get more." Of course, Joseph Smith served as the treasurer. Not only did this bank serve as a safe-house for money, but it also dabbled in the printing business—the printing of money. Smith claimed that this bank was ordained by God and that it was the safest of all banks. The printed money was said to be on the gold standard—backed by gold which he had in safe storage (probably the golden plates).

Smith later prophesied that the Kirtland Safety Society Bank would be so successful that it would swallow up all other banks.[98] But, needless to say, this never happened. The printing of money brought about the wrath of the U.S. Government and the bank went belly-up. It turned out that the Kirtland bank was not only started illegally, but a box of gold was nothing more that a box of bricks. And the prophecy—it too was a hoax. But a false prophecy was only a trivial item for Joseph. He had a much larger problem. With the collapse of the Bank, many people sought to regain their money from Joseph Smith.

> Thirteen suits were brought against him (Joseph) between June 1837 and April 1839, to collect sums totaling nearly $25,000. The damages asked amounted to almost $35,000. He was arrested seven times in four months, and his followers managed heroically to raise the $38,428 required for bail. Of the thirteen suits only

---

[98] *Millennial Star*, 19:43.

six were settled out of court—about $12,000 out of $25,000. In the other seven the creditors either were awarded damages or won them by default.

Joseph's debts to non-Mormons alone have been estimated to exceed $150,000.00.[99] Not only should this false prophecy warn Mormons about his divine calling, but his banking debts should tell a great deal about his character.

THE CIVIL WAR

Perhaps Smith's most famous prophecy is the one about the "Civil War." Smith predicted on December 25, 1832 that there would be a rebellious war beginning in South Carolina that would divide the nation from North to South.

> Verily, thus saith the Lord concerning the wars that will shortly come to pass, beginning at the rebellion of South Carolina, which will eventually terminate in the death and misery of many souls; and the time will come that war will be poured out upon all nations, beginning at this place. . . . and the Southern States will call on other nations, even the nation of Great Britain, as it is called, and they shall also call upon other nations, in order to defend themselves against other nations; and then war shall be poured out upon all nations. . . . And thus, with the sword and by bloodshed the inhabitants of the earth shall mourn; and with famine, and plague, and earthquake, and the thunder of heaven, and the fierce and vivid lightning also, shall the inhabitants of the earth be made to feel the wrath, and indignation, and chastening

---

[99] Taken from the Tanner's *Mormonism-Shadow or Reality?* p. 534, quoting Fawn Brodie and her work, *No Man Knows My History*, p. 199-202.

hand of an Almighty God, until the consumption decreed hath made a full end of all nations.[100]

What people do not realize is that similar predictions were made by newspapers across the country six months prior to Smith's prophecy. On July 14, 1832, President Andrew Jackson even alerted the nation that he expected war. All a person needs to do is review any good book on U.S. history or research newspapers from this time period to see that Smith was not the originator of this prediction. Even if Smith was totally unaware of the current events around him and actually "predicted" this event, he was greatly mistaken as to the extent of this war. Smith was convinced that this war would extend to all nations, and God's wrath would cause the destruction and the full end of all nations.

Joseph Smith is found errant in his predictions. He predicted that the event would happen shortly—it was not until 1861, thirty years later, that the war started. There were no "earthquakes," or "thunder of heaven," or "lightning" recorded during the events of the civil war. And the war did not spread across the "inhabitants of the earth," nor did it bring about "a full end of all nations."

And these are but a few examples of Joseph's false predictions. T. Harrison gives 32 false prophecies of Joseph Smith in his book, *Mormons Are Peculiar People.*

There can be no doubt why the L.D.S. church is ashamed of Joseph Smith. Even during his own lifetime many of his prophecies were proven false. When confronted with the problem of false predictions, Smith once said, "Some revelations are of God; some are of

---

[100] *Doctrine and Covenants*, 87:1-6.

men, and some are of the devil."[101]

Can you imagine a true prophet of God apologizing for an error? Smith needed to cover up his tracks. He was wrong more often than our own modern day astrologers such as Jeanne Dixon. Joseph must be rejected as a prophet, not only on the basis of his errors, but due to the fact that he never fulfilled the moral requirements, never possessed the godly characteristics, never attained the proper standards that the Bible sets forward for prophets. Joseph lacked humility, honesty, and integrity.[102]

Can there be any doubt as to whether Joseph Smith was a true prophet of God? The conclusion one must reach is that Joseph Smith is patently false. It is amazing that some Mormons do not seem to be troubled with these false prophecies and they refuse to see the implications of his error. Most continue to believe and teach that Joseph Smith was a prophet of God, and that his writings are God's infallible word. But some are not so blinded to the truth. No wonder they are "ashamed of Joseph."

---

[101] David Whitmer, *An Address to All Believers in Christ*, Richmond, Missouri, 1887, as quoted by Floyd C. McElveen, *The Mormon Illusion*, p. 35.

[102] These issues are dealt with more fully in other chapters of this book.

CHAPTER THIRTEEN

The Book of Mormon

The Mormon church not only places its faith in the person of Joseph Smith as their founder and prophet, but also in his supposed translation of the golden plates which resulted in the *Book of Mormon*. According to Joseph Smith, the *Book of Mormon* is

> . . . the most correct of any book on earth, and the keystone of our religion, and a man would be nearer to God by abiding its precepts, than by any other book.[103]

If it could be shown that the *Book of Mormon* was not what Joseph Smith said it was—then the total foundation of the Mormon church would be put in jeopardy.

---

[103] Joseph Smith, *History of the Church*, 4:461.

If a person believes that the *Book of Mormon* is "the most correct" book on earth, it would come as a shock to find that it was literally filled with errors and is historically unreliable. "The most correct" book on earth actually contained approximately seven mistakes on each side of each page.[104] How could this have been translated by the "gift and power of God" and yet be filled with so many errors? Did God make the mistakes? If God was helping in the translation, could He not have helped Joseph get it right?

A thinking person should ask some pointed questions like: Why are some of the stories in the *Book of Mormon* so outlandish? Why isn't the book historically, scientifically, and geographically accurate? Why is approximately one-third of this volume a quotation from the King James translation of the Bible (a translation that was not even available for 1211 years after the *Book of Mormon* was supposedly written)? Why does the *Book of Mormon* quote from Shakespeare? Why is there no archaeological evidence to support the *Book of Mormon*?

These questions (and others) pose major problems to the Mormon historians and the answers greatly disturb members of the Mormon church.

THE BOOK OF MORMON AND ARCHAEOLOGY

A huge blow is delivered to the reliability of the *Book of Mormon* when one learns that not one coin, not one city, not one river or people group has ever been found

---

[104] For more information on this subject, see my book *The Bible and Mormon Scriptures Compared.*

114

as mentioned in the *Book of Mormon*. This is difficult to stomach if you believe that the *Book of Mormon* is a historical document.

The *Book of Mormon* claims to portray the rise and development of two great civilizations. If this were the case, you would expect that archaeology and research would be able to turn up evidences for the *Book of Mormon*. As was previously stated, this is not the case! It should be observed that the *Book of Mormon* is neither accurate nor truthful when you consider the areas of archaeology and anthropology. Consider how embarrassing this is to Mormons!

Mormon missionaries often claim that the *Book of Mormon* is founded on solid archaeological evidence. I have personally encountered missionaries that claim that The Smithsonian Institution and other respectable organizations have even utilized the *Book of Mormon* as a guide in their research of ancient civilizations. But this is simply untrue! A spokesman from a major university put it this way.

> . . .I may say that I do not believe that there is a single thing of value concerning the prehistory of the American Indian in the *Book of Mormon* and I believe that the great majority of American archaeologists would agree with me. The book is untrue Biblically, historically and scientifically.[105]

There is not a single thing of value—not one shred of

---

[105]Excerpts from a letter addressed to the Rev. R. Odell Brown, pastor of the Hillcrest Methodist Church, Fredricksburg, Virginia from William Duncan Strong. This account can be found in Walter Martin's *Kingdom of the Cults*, pp. 184-185.

evidence found in support of the *Book of Mormon*! And this is not just one man's opinion, but the widespread feeling of archaeologists today. The Smithsonian Institution in Washington put it this way:

> . . . The Smithsonian Institution has never used the *Book of Mormon* in any way as a scientific guide. Smithsonian archaeologists see no direct connection between the archaeology of the New World and the subject matter of this book.[106]

The Smithsonian goes on to demonstrate seven areas in which the *Book of Mormon* is inconsistent with what we know about this civilization. Not only is the *Book of Mormon* unsubstantiated historically, it actually goes against what we know to be true of ancient America.

Even the National Geographic Society denies Mormon claims that the *Book of Mormon* is a historical account:

> With regard to the cities mentioned in the *Book of Mormon*, neither representatives of the National Geographic Society nor archaeologists connected with any other institution of equal prestige have ever used the *Book of Mormon* in locating historic ruins in Middle America or elsewhere.[107]

To my knowledge, there is not a single qualified archaeologist who will stand on behalf of the *Book of Mormon* as an accurate historical account. The evidence is so compelling that many former Mormon archaeologists have turned their backs on the Mormon church.

---

[106] Walter Martin, *Kingdom of the Cults*, pp. 184-185.

[107] This letter and others like it are reproduced in Jerry and Marian Bodine, *Whom Can You Trust?* p. 13. Citing letter of Mr. Hammersen to Mr. Gregory R. Shannon, May 29, 1978.

Compare this with the accuracy and legitimacy of the Bible and you will see why the Mormons are "sort of embarrassed by Joseph Smith."

An examination of the evidence would lead any thinking person to ask, "If the *Book of Mormon* is not a historical book based on real events of ancient history, what is it? In 1983, Vernal Holley went a long way in answering this question.

THE GEOGRAPHICAL SETTING FOR THE BOOK OF MORMON

Vernal Holley wrote a very fine little book called, *Book of Mormon Authorship: A Closer Look*. His basic premise is that the *Book of Mormon* is not at all an ancient document translated by Joseph Smith, but that it must have been a contemporary novel written by Solomon Spaulding.[108] He comes to this conclusion based on a multitude of evidence. One of the basic reasons for this conclusion is that the *Book of Mormon* is parallel in so many ways to one of Spaulding's writings.

One section of Holley's book seems to break virgin soil. He almost certainly has located the geographical place where the author of the *Book of Mormon* centers his account. Holley has taken a map of Southern Canada and the Northern United States where the two countries join near Lake Erie and Lake Ontario. This area includes Ohio, New York, and Pennsylvania. He has then plotted the events of the *Book of Mormon* on this modern-day map. (Remember that the *Book of Mormon* claims to be an ancient book which tracks the migration of three people groups through North, Central and South America).

Holley has plotted the "land northward" and the "land southward" on this map of the Northern United States. He shows the "Sea West" and the "Sea East." He has pinpointed the various Mormon cities and valleys as best he could from the narratives of the *Book of Mormon*.

By so doing, it becomes clear that the person who wrote the *Book of Mormon* knew the modern areas well and wrote a fictitious account based on the geographical setting of which he was familiar. If this is true, the *Book of Mormon* is nothing more than a novel of an ancient civilization with a geographical setting based on modern cities, rivers, and geographical areas from North America. It is not a record of ancient historical events which took place in South and Central America.

Here is a partial list of names and places from the *Book of Mormon* compared with modern names and places.[109]

---

[109] Vernal Holley, *Book of Mormon Authorship: A Closer Look*

Modern Maps	Mormon Maps
Agathe, Saint	Ogath
Alma	Alma, Valley of
Angola	Angola
Antrim	Antum
Antioch	Anti-Anti
Boaz	Boaz
Conner	Comner
Ephrem, Saint	Ephraim, Hill
Hellam	Helam
Jacobsburg	Jacobbugath
Jerusalem	Jerusalem
Jordon	Jordon
Kishkiminetas	Kishkumen
Lehigh	Lehi
Matua	Manti
Monroe	Moroni
Minoa	Minon
Moraviantown	Morianton
Morin	Moron
Noah Lake	Noah, Land of
Oneida	Onidah
Oneida Castle	Onidah, Hill
Omer	Omner
Rama	Ramah
Ripple Lake	Ripliancum, Waters of
Sodom	Sidom
Shiloh	Shilom
Shurbrook	Shurr
Tecumseh/Tenecum	Teancum

Is it just a coincidence that supposed ancient cities of South America so resemble modern places? Why is it that the *Book of Mormon* has been found to have a geographical setting near the Great Lakes between the United States and Canada when it supposedly occurred in ancient times in North, Central, and South America? Why does the *Book of Mormon* use only slightly changed names of modern places? Could it be that the *Book of Mormon* isn't really an ancient manuscript? Certainly it is not!

MODERN CONTROVERSIES IN THE BOOK OF MORMON

It should also be observed that the *Book of Mormon* deals with "modern" religious controversies of the day. In 1831, Alexander Campbell pointed this out in the *Millennial Harbinger,*

> This prophet Smith, through his stone spectacles, wrote on the plates of Nephi, in his Book of Mormon, every error and almost every truth discussed in New York for the last ten years. He decides all the great controversies; —infant baptism, ordination, the trinity, regeneration, repentance, justification, the fall of man, the atonement, transubstantiation, fasting, penance, church government, religious experience, the call to the ministry, the general resurrection, eternal punishment, who may baptize, and even the question of free masonary [sic], republican government, and the rights of man.[110]

Why does the *Book of Mormon* cover all these "current" issues of the day? The most obvious answer is that the account is not a historical document. The facts cer-

---

[110] Alexander Campbell, February 1831, p. 93.

tainly lead one to know that the writer of the *Book of Mormon* used modern existing places, names, and current topics of discussion to write a novel about fictitious people and events.

SOLOMON SPAULDING AND THE BOOK OF MORMON

As mentioned earlier, Holley's basic premise is that the *Book of Mormon* is not at all an ancient document translated by Joseph Smith, but that it was a contemporary novel written by Solomon Spaulding. He is not alone in his thinking. It is worth mentioning that Solomon Spaulding had written a novel which bears remarkable similarity to the *Book of Mormon*.

According to Henry Lake (Solomon's business partner), he and Spaulding planned on printing Solomon's novel, "Manuscript Found," but for various reasons, they had been unable to do so. Years later, Henry Lake recognized parts of the *Book of Mormon* as being from Spaulding's book.

I formed a copartnership with Solomon Spaulding, for the purpose of rebuilding a forge which he had commenced a year or two before. He very frequently read to me from a manuscript which he was writing which he entitled the "Manuscript Found," and which he represented as being found in this town. I spent many hours in hearing him read said writings, and became well acquainted with its contents. . . . This book represented the American Indians as the descendants of the lost tribes, gave account of their leaving Jerusalem, their contentions and wars, which were many and great. One time, when he was reading to me the tragic account of Laban, I pointed out to him what I considered an inconsistency, which he promised to correct: but by referring to the Book of Mormon, I find, to my surprise, that it stands there just as he read it to me then. Some months ago, I borrowed the Golden Bible, put it into my pocket, carried it home, and thought no more of it. About a week after, my wife found the book in my coat pocket, as it hung up, and commenced reading it aloud as I lay upon the bed. She had not read twenty minutes, till I was astonished to find the same passages in it that Spaulding had read to me more than twenty years before, from his "Manuscript Found." Since that, I have more fully examined the said Golden Bible, and have no hesitation in saying that the historical part of it is principally, if not wholly, taken from the "Manuscript Found" . . . Spaulding left here in 1812 . . . I never heard any more from him or his writings, till I saw them in the Book of Mormon.

(Signed)
Henry Lake[111]

To further prove this case, a person needs only look to other sworn testimonies of Spaulding's family, his co-workers, and numerous other witnesses. Solomon Spaulding's brother John provides one of these testimonies:

I have recently read the Book of Mormon and to my great surprise I find it nearly the same historical matter, names, & c., as they were in my brother's writings. . . . and according to the best of my recollection and belief, it is the same as my brother Solomon wrote, with the exception of the religious matter. By what means it has fallen into the hands of Joseph Smith, Jr., I am unable to determine.

(Signed)
John Spaulding[112]

---

[111] Eber D. Howe, *History of Mormonism*, pp. 282-283.
[112] *Ibid.*, pp. 278-280.

John N. Miller, an associate of Solomon Spaulding, was also familiar with Spaulding's writings.

> I have recently examined the Book of Mormon, and find in it the writings of Solomon Spaulding, from beginning to end, but mixed up with Scripture and other religious matter, which I did not meet with in "Manuscript Found." Many of the passages in the Mormon book are verbatim from Spaulding, and others in part. . . .
>
> (Signed)
> John N. Miller[113]

Many others have given similar testimonies and much has been written on this subject. Those who have written come to similar conclusions—Joseph Smith did not receive golden plates from an angel of God, but plagiarized a stolen manuscript and fraudulently distributed it as a companion scripture to the Bible. Although many people agree that Joseph Smith plagiarized from other manuscripts, not everyone is in agreement that it entirely originated from Solomon Spaulding.

OTHER PARALLEL WRITINGS TO THE BOOK OF MORMON

The plot here thickens. Solomon Spaulding was not the only person to have preceded Joseph in writing an account of the Ancient Americas. Ethan Smith wrote a book entitled *View of the Hebrews* which contains over 120 parallels to the *Book of Mormon*. Eighteen of these parallels are so striking that one must conclude that information was shared between the *Book of Mormon* and *View of the Hebrews*. The problem is that Ethan

---

[113]*Ibid.*, pp. 278-280.

Smith's work was copyrighted five years before the *Book of Mormon* was printed. What should we conclude about the similarities between these three books *(Manuscript Found, View of the Hebrews,* and the *Book of Mormon)*? There must have been some plagiarism. One must point out that of these three books, the *Book of Mormon* stands last in chronological order of printing.

But the problems with the *Book of Mormon* don't stop here. No fewer than eight other books bear a resemblance to the *Book of Mormon*. Seven of these eight books predate the *Book of Mormon*. They are:

1. *Origen de los Indios del Nuevo Mundo, e Indias Occidentales* by Gregorio Garcia. Second Edition. Valencia: Pedro Patricio Mey, 1607, 1729.

2. *The History of the American Indians* by James Adair. London: Edward and Charles Dilly, 1775.

3. *An Essay upon the Propagation of the Gospel*, by Charles Crawford. Philadelphia: J. Gales, 1799. Second edition, 1801.

4. *A Star in the West; or A Humble Attempt to Discover the Long Lost Tribes of Israel*, by Elias Boudinot. Trenton: D. Fenton, S. Hutchinson, and J. Dunham, 1816.

5. *View of the Hebrews*, by Ethan Smith. Poultney: Smith and Shute, 1823.

6. *The Wonders of Nature and Providence, Displayed*, by Josiah Priest. Albany: E. and E. Hosford, 1825.

7. *A View of the American Indians*, by Israel Worsley. London: R. Hunter, 1828.

8. *Antiquities of Mexico*, by Lord Kingsborough. Seven Volumes. London: Augustine Aglio, 1830.

The point is this—the major thesis of the *Book of Mormon* was very well covered long before Joseph purported his supposed "translation." Not only had the major thesis been a well discussed topic, but two writers had actually written accounts very similar (identical in many instances) to the *Book of Mormon* years before Joseph came on the scene. This would not be a problem except that the accounts are purely fictionalized and bear no resemblance to history. The accounts were nothing more that popularized stories and fables of the day that had no basis in fact. There is no longer a question as to whether Joseph Smith fabricated his translation of ancient plates and copied from earlier works that were available to him—there can be no doubt he did.

The only question centers around that of plagiarism! "Whom did Joseph plagiarize, Solomon Spaulding, Ethan Smith, or both?" In either case, Joseph Smith stands third in line (or eighth) for this information.

A thinking person must resolve the questions asked in this chapter? Let's go back through these questions and insert what seems to be the appropriate answer:

"The *Book of Mormon* was based on a fictitious novel and is not a historical account."

Remember the questions?

Why isn't the *Book of Mormon* historically, scientifically, and geographically accurate? Why does it contain so many errors? (Insert the answer we have been discussing!) Because it was based on a fictitious novel and is not a historical account.

Why is it approximately one-third a quotation from the King James translation of the Bible—a translation that was not even available for 1211 years after the *Book of Mormon* was allegedly finished? Why does the *Book of Mormon* quote Shakespeare? Because the *Book of Mormon* is based on a modern fictitious novel written centuries after the King James Bible was translated and written by a man who had access to the writings of William Shakespeare.

Why is there no archaeological evidence to support the *Book of Mormon*? Because the *Book of Mormon* is based on a fictitious novel and is not at all, nor was ever meant to be a historical account.

Why does the *Book of Mormon* discuss modern problems of the day and age in which it was published? Because it was a modern work!

A thinking person must come to these conclusions. Wouldn't you be ashamed of your "prophet" if you found that he hadn't uncovered an ancient manuscript, but was a thief, a plagiarist, a story teller, and a liar? Yes, there is good reason to play down Joseph Smith and his work.

CHAPTER FOURTEEN

"Doctrines"

The Mormon church had its beginning in an area where three other cultist groups also originated. The Seventh Day Adventists, Jehovah's Witnesses, and Christian Science churches all begin within a radius of two hundred miles and within fifty years of each other.

This was a day of religious discussion and often religious ignorance. Many difficult biblical passages were a part of common discussion among Christian people of that day and age. Such subjects as baptism for the dead, preaching to the spirits in prison, and the third heaven, were matters of common and often heated discussions.

Since the Bible sometimes seemed unclear, especially to those without proper training, these discussions went on and on without a satisfactory conclusion; that is, until Joseph Smith came on the scene.

Joseph Smith spoke authoritatively and conclusively about these things. A thorough study of his answers demonstrate that he also knew little of theology or history.

In view of the circumstances, it is not surprising to find false doctrines springing up around the difficult passages of the Bible. The Mormon doctrine of "three heavens" typifies an unscholarly attempt to explain what on the surface seems to be a difficult passage. The doctrine of baptism for people already dead came out of another such passage in 1 Corinthians 15:29.

Preaching to "spirits in prison" helped Joseph Smith devise the doctrine that Jesus preached to the American Indians, and that the Gospel message was taken to people already in hell.

It might be helpful at this juncture to discuss a few of the doctrines of the Mormon church.

MEN MAY BECOME GODS:

Mormonism teaches that all people preexisted eternally as "intelligences"—blobs of knowledge that are in a state of flux, floating around the universe. The *Book of Abraham* talks about this state of preexistence.

> Now the Lord had shown unto me . . . the intelligences that were organized before the world was; and among all these there were many of the noble and great ones.[114]

---

[114] *Book of Abraham*, 3:22-23.

128

These "intelligences," according to Mormon doctrine were in existence[115] before the world was created and are awaiting the time when they can become "spirit children." After Elohim and his wife have physical relations, these intelligences are able to take their place as a spirit baby and then await the opportunity to come to earth when a physical body is formed for them. Even as spirits, man was working towards eternal progression.

> Although we do not know how long we existed as spirits before coming to earth, we know that it must have been a place of growth and testimony, where we had the power to make our own decisions and to progress.[116]

According to Mormon doctrine, man is working through a four step process: 1) He is originally an intelligence, 2) then he is fashioned as preexistent spirit being, 3) next, he is able to come to earth and inhabit a body when human sexual intercourse provides a residence, and finally, 4) man continues the process on earth of working towards exaltation or godhood.[117]

The *Doctrine and Covenants* suggests not only that we can become a god, but that we can surpass God.

> . . . and they shall pass by the angels, and the gods, which are set there, to their exaltation and glory . . . Then shall they be gods . . . then shall they be above all, because all things are subject unto them. Then shall they be gods, because they have all power, and angels are subject to them.[118]

---

[115] *Moses* 3:5 states that every creature upon the earth existed spiritually before it was created physically.

[116] *Principles of the Gospel*, p. 237.

[117] Some of their prophets, like Brigham Young, suggested that this process started on earth when God Himself came to earth as Adam to propagate the earth.

[118] *Doctrine and Covenants*, 132:19-20.

But what does the Bible clearly say?

Thus says the Lord, the King of Israel and his Redeemer, the Lord of hosts: I am the first and I am the last, and there is no God besides Me.[119]

You are My witnesses, declares the Lord, and My servant whom I have chosen, in order that you may know and believe Me, and understand that I am He. Before Me there was no God formed, and there will be none after Me.[120]

I am the Lord, and there is no other; Besides Me there is no God . . . .[121]

. . . One God and Father of all who is over all and through all and in all.[122]

JESUS WAS NOT BORN OF THE VIRGIN MARY:

Mormons teach that Jesus was merely the "Firstborn" of Elohim, and is only different from the rest of mankind in that He preceded the rest of the spirit babies in heaven. Mormons teach that Elohim had physical relations with Mary to produce the body which Jesus would inhabit.

Jesus, our elder brother, was begotten in the flesh. . . . Now, remember from this time forth, and for ever, that Jesus Christ was not begotten by the Holy Ghost.[123]

The birth of the Saviour was as natural as are the births of our children; it was the result of natural action. He partook of flesh and blood—was begotten of his Father, as we were of our fathers.[124]

---

[119] Isaiah 44:6
[120] Isaiah 43:10
[121] Isaiah 45:5
[122] Ephesians 4:6
[123] Brigham Young, *Journal of Discourses*, 1:51.
[124] *Ibid.*, 8:115.

But what does the Bible clearly say? Jesus was born of the virgin Mary and was conceived of the Holy Spirit.

> And Joseph arose from his sleep, and did as the angel of the Lord commanded him, and took her as his wife, and kept her a virgin until she gave birth to a Son; and he called His name Jesus.[125]

> Therefore the Lord Himself will give you a sign: Behold, a virgin will be with child and bear a son, and she will call His name Immanuel.[126]

> Behold, an angel of the Lord appeared to him in a dream, saying, "Joseph, son of David, do not be afraid to take Mary as your wife; for that which has been conceived in her is of the Holy Spirit". . . . And Joseph arose from his sleep, and did as the angel of the Lord commanded him, and took her as his wife, and kept her a virgin until she gave birth to a Son; and he called His name Jesus.[127]

THERE ARE SEVERAL HEAVENS:

Le Grand Richards, Mormon apostle states:

> One of the greatest errors in the teachings of the Christian religions is the doctrine of one heaven and one hell, so that all who fail to go to heaven are sent to hell where they share and share alike.[128]

Mormonism teaches there are three principal heavens—the celestial is the highest, followed by the terrestrial and telestial heavens. These heavens are earned

---

[125] Matthew 1:24, 25

[126] Isaiah 7:14

[127] Matthew 1:20, 24,25

[128] LeGrand Richards, *A Marvelous Work and A Wonder,* p. 253.

and represent degrees of privilege and reward. Mormon doctrine suggests that "Man's rewards will vary as much as men themselves vary in righteousness."[129] The *Doctrine and Covenants* even suggests that rewards are granted upon the basis of intellect and diligence.

> If a person gains more knowledge and intelligence in this life through his diligence and obedience than another, he will have so much advantage in the world to come.[130]

But true salvation is not found simply in making it to heaven, it is making it to the highest heaven where one can be exalted to godhood.

> Man has within him the power . . . to develop in truth, faith, wisdom, and all the virtues, that eventually he shall become like the Father and the Son. . . . Thus it is destined that those who are worthy . . . would be heirs of the Father's kingdom, possessing the same attributes in their perfection, as the Father and the Son now possess.[131]

But what does the Bible say? While the Bible does mention "being caught up to the third heaven" in 2 Corinthians 12:2, it in no way resembles what Joseph Smith or the Mormons would have us make of it. Those who have carefully studied theology and the Bible (or even the Greek thinking of the day) know that the three heavens were:

1) Where the birds fly—"The birds of the heavens."
2) Where the stars and galaxies are—"The stars of the heavens."

---

[129] *Principles of the Gospel*, p. 201.
[130] *Doctrine and Covenants*, 130:19.
[131] *Doctrines of Salvation*, 2;13, 35.

3) Where God is—"The third heaven."

Being caught up to the third heaven was simply Paul's way of clarifying that he had been in the very presence of God. Paul is not making a theological statement about various "rewards" of heaven but simply stating that he visited with God and has some words of importance to share.

Throughout the pages of the Bible it speaks of but one heaven and one hell, of one punishment and one reward. The problem with LeGrand Richards' conclusion, as well as the doctrine of Mormonism, is found in their premise. Mormons believe that a person "earns" his degree of heaven. As Christians we see the fallacy of this proposition. Contrary to Mormon teaching, the Bible teaches that none of us deserve heaven. No one can be "good enough." As one person so ably put it, "being good enough just isn't good enough." In truth, all of us are deserving of eternal punishment and no one is deserving of heaven. But the beauty of the message of Christianity is that Christ has paid the penalty of sin, and there is a heaven for those who have accepted his gift of grace.

The Prophet Isaiah put this rather plainly when he said:

> All of us like sheep have gone astray, each of us has turned to his own way; but the Lord has caused the iniquity of us all to fall on Him.[132]

---

[132] Isaiah 53:6

HELL IS NOT ETERNAL:

In Mormon theology, hell (for most of its occupants) is only a temporary residence where a person can pay the penalty of their sins. After receiving the due punishment for their error, the person will be raised up to inherit a degree of heaven. The "sons of perdition" are the only people who will not have the opportunity to reach heaven. They are principally composed of Mormons who have denied the faith, and might possibly include a few adulterers and murderers.

But what does the Bible say?

And these will go away into eternal punishment, but the righteous into eternal life.[133]

---

[133] Matthew 25:46

The duration of heaven and hell are thus the same. Jesus makes it very clear that many will be lost.

> Enter by the narrow gate; for the gate is wide, and the way is broad that leads to destruction, and many are those who enter by it.[134]

For those whose name is not found in the Book of Life, hell will be eternal punishment.

> But for the . . . unbelieving and abominable and murders and immoral persons and sorcerers and idolaters and all liars, their part will be in the lake that burns with fire and brimstone.[135]

THERE ARE OTHER WORLDS OVER WHICH CELESTIAL GODS AND THEIR WIVES RULE:

Mormonism would have us believe that there are an infinite number of gods and limitless earths on which the gods can reign. Elohim is said to be the "god" of this earth ONLY and is not a "god" of the whole universe. When man works his way up to godhood, he in turn will receive an earth to rule. Jesus, while on earth was merely on the path to exaltation, much like Joseph Smith.

Exaltation is said to be the very essence of why we are put on earth. To deny the possibility of becoming a god is to deny the fundamental truth around which Mormonism revolves.

> The first great principle that ought to occupy the attention of mankind . . . is the principle of improvement.

---

[134] Matthew 7:13
[135] Revelation 21:8

135

The principle of increase, of exaltation, of adding to that we already possess, is the grand moving principle.[136]

But what does the Bible say? The Bible teaches throughout its pages that there is only one God. How could any man then become God? It is horrendous heresy. The delusion of Mormonism that we can become like God has been around since the beginning of time. If you remember, this was the very ploy of Satan in the garden!

And the serpent said to the woman, "You surely shall not die! For God knows that in the day you eat from it your eyes will be opened, and you will be like God."[137]

The Bible teaches us that we are to turn to God, not into God.

SINNERS WHO DIE WITHOUT JESUS HAVE ANOTHER CHANCE TO BE SAVED AFTER THEY DIE:

Mormons go to great lengths researching genealogies in order to be baptized for those who failed to do so themselves. A person can be spared from purgatory if some good L.D.S. person will be baptized for them.

But what does the Bible say? Again it is quite clear on the subject of what happens after death.

And inasmuch as it is appointed for men to die once and after this comes judgment.[138]

---

[136] *Discourses of Brigham Young*, p. 87.
[137] Genesis 3:4, 5
[138] Hebrews 9:27

He who has believed and has been baptized shall be saved; but he who has disbelieved shall be condemned.[139]

Not everyone who says to Me, "Lord, Lord," will enter the kingdom of heaven; but he who does the will of My Father who is in heaven. Many will say to Me on that day, "Lord, Lord, did we not prophesy in Your name, and in Your name cast out demons, and in Your name perform many miracles?" And then I will declare to them, "I never knew you; depart from Me, you who practice lawlessness."[140]

SATAN AND DEMONS ARE OUR SPIRIT BROTHERS:

Satan is the brother of Jesus as well as a spirit brother of all men and women on earth. We were all formed by Elohim and his wife. But Satan led a rebellion in the spirit world against Elohim. Elohim declared that they would not be able to inherit earthly bodies thus resigning them to life as evil spirits.

And there stood one among them that was like unto God, and he said unto those who were with him: We will go down, for there is space there, and we will take these materials, and we will make an earth whereon these may dwell . . . And the Lord said: Whom shall I send? And one answered like unto the Son of Man: Here am I, send me. And another answered and said: Here am I, send me. And the Lord said: I will send the first. And the second was angry . . . and, at that day, many followed him.[141]

---

[139] Mark 16:16
[140] Matthew 7:21-23
[141] The *Book of Abraham*, 3:24-28.

But what does the Bible say? Jesus is always spoken of as "The only begotten Son of God." Most everyone is familiar with John 3:16:

> For God so loved the world, that He gave His only begotten Son, that whoever believes in Him should not perish, but have eternal life.

SIN IS NOT REALLY SIN:

Mormonism does not hold an orthodox view of sin. Sin is defined as anything that tends to prevent or hinder the development of the human soul. In other words, sin is whatever keeps one from progressing to godhood. Thus, Adam and Eve did not commit a sin in the garden—they actually did us a favor.

> If Adam had not eaten of the forbidden fruit . . . he and Eve would have remained unable to bring other spirits into the world as their children. . . . Thus, the purpose of this earth's creation would have been frustrated. . . . By partaking of the forbidden fruit, Adam was able to obey the commandment to bring forth children, and he also made it possible for us to fulfill our purpose on earth to learn through our experiences the good from evil: "And now, behold, if Adam had not transgressed he would not have fallen . . . wherefore they would have remained in a state of innocence, having no joy, for they knew no misery; doing no good, for they knew no sin." (2 Nephi 2:22-23.)[142]

"The Fall of Man" was not only beneficial, but necessary for mankind to achieve godhood. In Mormon theology, it is the fall of man which provides Adam and

---

[142] *Principles of the Gospel*, p. 167.

138

Eve with flesh and blood. Since Mormons believe that it is impossible to progress without a physical body, the fall was necessary to start the progression. The Mormon scriptures actually depict the "Fall of Man" as a festive occasion. The *Book of Moses* tells us that Adam and Eve were glad that they ate from the forbidden tree in the garden.

> And in that day Adam blessed God and was filled, and began to prophesy concerning all the families of the earth, saying: Blessed be the name of God for because of my transgression my eyes are opened, and in this life I shall have joy, and in the flesh I shall see God. And Eve, his wife, heard all these things and was glad, saying: Were it not for our transgression we never should have had seed, and never should have known good and evil, and the joy of our redemption, and the eternal life which God giveth unto all the obedient. And Adam and Eve blessed the name of God . . . .[143]

But what does the Bible say? Sin is an act which is contrary to the will of God. The book of James even tells us that a person can sin without doing anything—if he knows he should have done something.[144] In the Bible, Adam and Eve were told not to eat of the fruit of the tree in the middle of the garden, and yet they ate it.[145] It was a deliberate act against the will of God. It was a sin! The Bible clearly calls it this. Read the fifth chapter of Romans.

Therefore, just as through one man (Adam) sin entered

---

[143] *Moses*, 5:11-13.
[144] James 4:17
[145] Genesis 3:3, 6

into the world, and death through sin, and so death spread to all men, because all sinned.[146]

The Bible squarely places blame on Adam and Eve for disobeying God and listening to the voice of the serpent—this is in stark contrast to the Mormon account. The Bible also pictures a significantly different picture as to the events in the Garden of Eden. In the biblical account, Adam and Eve are not found rejoicing like the Mormons would have us believe. Read the story found in Genesis chapter three and determine yourself whether or not it was a joyous occasion.

> And the Lord said to the woman, "What is this you have done?" And the woman said, "The serpent deceived me, and I ate." And the Lord God said . . . "I will greatly multiply your pain in childbirth . . ." Then to Adam He said, "Because you have listened to the voice of your wife, and have eaten from the tree about which I commanded you, saying, 'You shall not eat from it;' Cursed is the ground because of you; In toil you shall eat of it all the days of your life. Both thorns and thistles it shall grow for you; and you shall eat the plants of the field; By the sweat of your face you shall eat bread, till you return to the ground, because from it you were taken; for you are dust, and to dust you shall return."[147]

THE SECOND COMING OF CHRIST AND JOSEPH:

Mormons do speak of the second coming of the "earth god," Jesus. But they also refer to the second coming of Joseph Smith.

---

[146] Romans 5:12
[147] Genesis 3:13-19

We have not set our feet to the race for any other purpose than to follow him and run through; for he is our leader and will be our leader, temporally and spiritually, from this time forth. When Joseph comes again, will brother Brigham be removed? No, never.[148]

Joseph Smith holds the keys of this last dispensation, and is now engaged behind the vail in the great work of the last days . . . no man or woman will ever enter into the celestial kingdom of God without the consent of Joseph Smith . . . He holds the keys of that kingdom . . . he rules triumphantly, for he gained full power and a glorious victory over the power of Satan . . . He reigns there as supreme a being in his sphere, capacity, and calling as God does in heaven . . . Joseph Smith, junior, will again be on this earth dictating plans and calling forth his brethren . . . .[149]

Brigham Young suggest that it was Joseph Smith who conquered the power of Satan, who now reigns supremely, and who is coming back to call forth his people.

But what does the Bible clearly say? Acts depicts Christ ascending into heaven with the followers of Jesus gathered all around. And while they were gazing into the sky, two angels said:

Men of Galilee, why do you stand looking into the sky? This Jesus, who has been taken up from you into heaven, will come in just the same way as you have watched Him go into heaven.[150]

If Jesus is to come in the same way as he left, it would be without Joseph. When the event does happen, 2 Peter

[148] President Heber C. Kimball, *Journal of Discourses*, 5:19.
[149] Brigham Young, *Journal of Discourses*, 7:238-239.
[150] Acts 1:11

tells us that it will be like a thief in the night and that we need to always be prepared.[151] 2 Peter mentions another future event which might be more appropriately tied to Joseph.

> But false prophets also arose among the people, just as there will also be false teachers among you, who will secretly introduce destructive heresies, even denying the Master who bought them, bringing swift destruction upon themselves. And many will follow their sensuality, and because of them the way of the truth will be maligned; and in their greed they will exploit you with false words.[152]

There are numerous other doctrines to which we could turn our attention. The Mormons teach marriage for time and eternity, heavenly polygamy, and sex in heaven. They teach that salvation is attainable through good works, and that some races are cursed by God. They also have very twisted doctrines about elders and deacons and unorthodox teachings about the Lord's Supper.

These doctrines of the Mormon church show basic ignorance of theology and the Bible. They are a strange mixture of Christianity, the Masonic Lodge, and paganism. Most of these doctrines are grounded in the teachings of their prophet Joseph Smith and should be a matter of embarrassment.

A CLASSIC EXAMPLE OF FALSE DOCTRINE

It might be interesting to follow in depth, one more Mormon doctrine to demonstrate more fully why they

---

[151] 2 Peter 3:10
[152] 2 Peter 2:1-3

really are ashamed of Joseph. Let's examine their teaching about black, African people.

Certainly there is no biblical foundation that any black person was cursed by God. Two passages have been given as proof-texts by southern, white Americans to seek to justify their keeping of slaves.

The first of these passages is one that speaks of the "Mark of Cain."[153] Slave holders suggested that the mark assigned to Cain was dark skin.

I remember listening to a talk-radio station in Salt Lake City, Utah while they were discussing this very issue. During this program, an elderly lady called the radio station. Her inflection and enunciation gave the distinct impression that she was of African-American descent. Her response to their accusation that God turned Cain black was rather humorous: "We'se believe God turned Cain white." Certainly she had as much evidence for her point of view as does the one who says God turned Cain black.

The second passage speaks of a curse being placed on the son of Ham.[154] Mormons suggest that Canaan was turned black because of his father's wickedness—Ham had seen his father's nakedness and laughed at him. It takes little research to find that Canaan, the one cursed, became the father of the Canaanites, not the black races of Africa.

There is no biblical evidence of a cursed race. But this doesn't slow down the bigotry found in Mormonism. There is a lot said about "the cursed race" in Mormon doctrine. The *Book of Mormon* is the first to bring up this perverted teaching.

---

[153] Genesis 4:15
[154] Genesis 9:22-25

And he had caused the cursing to come upon them, yea, even a sore cursing, because of their iniquity. For behold, they had hardened their hearts against him, that they had become like unto a flint; wherefore, as they were white, and exceeding fair and delightsome, that they might not be enticing unto my people the Lord God did cause a skin of blackness to come upon them. And thus saith the Lord God: I will cause that they shall be loathsome unto thy people, save they shall repent of their iniquities.[155]

Again the *Book of Mormon* says:

And the skins of the Lamanites were dark, according to the mark which was set upon their fathers, which was a curse upon them because of their transgression and their rebellion against their brethren, who consisted of Nephi, Jacob, and Joseph, and Sam, who were just and holy men.[156]

The Mormon church has taught,

Not only was Cain called upon to suffer, but because of his wickedness he became the father of an inferior race.[157]

Again,

Their skin is quite black, their hair woolly and black, their intelligence stunted, and they appear never to have arisen from the most savage state of barbarian.[158]

The words of Brigham Young come to mind,

---

[155] *Book of Mormon*, 2 Nephi 5:21-22.
[156] *Ibid.*, Alma 3:6.
[157] Joseph F. Smith, *The Way to Perfection*, p. 101.
[158] *The Juvenile Instructor*, Vol. 3, p. 157.

Shall I tell you the law of God in regard to the African race? If the white man who belongs to the chosen seeds mixes his blood with the seed of Cain, the penalty, under the law of God, is death on the spot. This will always be so.[159]

This has left the Mormon church quite ashamed of Joseph Smith and rightly so. Certainly this gives us good reason to doubt the credibility of a whole religious system that bases its dogmas on such a prophet.

Modern L.D.S. prophets have struggled with this issue. For example, Harold B. Lee, Prophet of the L.D.S. church, said in an interview by John Keahey for the *Salt Lake Tribune*,

We must believe in the justice of God, the Negro will achieve full status; we're just waiting for that time . . . It is ironic we are called 'racist,' in the light of all the work we have done with minorities throughout the world.[160]

An advertisement placed in the *Salt Lake Tribune*, Sunday February 24, 1980, by Modern Microfilm discusses the dilemma the church faces because of Joseph Smith's and Brigham Young's racist teachings.

David Briscoe and George Buck refer to June 9, 1978 as "Black Friday" because this was the day that Mormon leaders announced the death of the anti-black doctrine.[161]

Prior to this time, blacks of African lineage were not allowed to hold the Priesthood nor go through the

---

[159] *The Journal of Discourses*, p. 110.
[160] The *Salt Lake Tribune*, Sunday, September 24, 1972.
[161] See *Utah Holiday*, July 1978, p. 3.

temple—even if they had lived exemplary lives. The Mormon position concerning blacks was clearly stated in a letter written by the First Presidency on July 17, 1947:

> From the days of the Prophet Joseph even until now, it has been the doctrine of the Church, never questioned by any of the Church leaders, that the Negroes are not entitled to the full blessings of the Gospel.

Apostle McConkie wrote the following in 1958:

> Negroes in this life are denied the priesthood; under no circumstances can they hold this delegation of authority from the Almighty. The gospel message of salvation is not carried affirmatively to them . . . Negroes are not equal with other races where the receipt of certain spiritual blessings are concerned . . . .[162]

During the controversy surrounding the decision to grant blacks the Priesthood a Larry J. Hall wrote:

> On June 1, 1978 the First Presidency and the Twelve Apostles of the L.D.S. Church permitted Negroes to hold the Priesthood.[163]

The Priesthood is regarded as the ultimate authority by which men are empowered to carry on their ministry here on the earth. Mormons claim that without the authority of the Priesthood none of their ordinances would have any value in the sight of God.

Previously, blacks were not allowed to hold the Priesthood because of the "curse." The Mormon

---

[162] Bruce McConkie, *Mormon Doctrine*, p. 477.
[163] News clipping from the *News Review*, June, 1978.

Prophet Brigham Young declared that having one drop of Negro blood was sufficient to bring a person under the curse and bar him from the Priesthood.

Brigham Young, in true prophetic style, anticipated the day when the church would reverse itself on this matter. He declared that if the time ever came when the Presidency and the Twelve Apostles should meet and confer the Priesthood on Negroes, immediately the Priesthood would be taken from the church and the curse be given in its place.

Prophet Young declared:

> . . . the First Presidency, the Twelve, the High counsel, the Bishopric, and all the Elders of Israel, suppose we summon them to appear here, and here declare that it is right to mingle our seed, with the black race of Cain, that they shall come in with us and be partakers with us of all the blessings God has given us. On that very day, and hour we should do so, the Priesthood is taken from this Church and Kingdom and God leaves us to our fate. The moment we consent to mingle with the seed of Cain the Church must go to destruction,—we should receive the curse which has been placed upon the seed of Cain, and never more be numbered with the children of Adam who are heirs to the Priesthood until that curse be removed.(Brigham Young's Addresseses, Feb. 5, 1852, ms.d. 1234, Box 48, folder 3). Located in the L.D.S. Church Historical Department, Salt Lake City.

You see it is apparent that the L.D.S. church needs to be ashamed of its prophets who give false and misleading information, not to mention a doctrine that is full of prejudice.

THE DICHOTOMY FACING MORMONS TODAY

Joseph L. Jensen, Chairman of the Star of Truth Publishing, is struggling with what to do with all the doctrines of the past. He typifies the struggle that is going on within the L.D.S. church. His article is entitled, "Shall We Excommunicate Joseph Smith?"

The questions raised by Mr. Jensen must be running through the minds of many Mormons today. How can a clear-thinking person justify the things that are taught by the early founders of Mormonism?

How could Joseph Smith be a prophet of God and be wrong so often? How can the church teach that an immoral and fallible man can be a true prophet of God? How can the church reverse the very teachings of the man who founded the church? How can the church change "everlasting" covenants?

This dilemma is a tough one for the L.D.S. people. Is Mr. Jensen a typical L.D.S.? His article quoted below certainly sounds like it. Jensen wrestles with the problem of what is, and what is not, scripture. If the Mormon writings are truly scripture how can they be changed at every whim of current social change and pressure?

Mr. Jensen's article is rather lengthy, but it so clearly illustrates the current dilemma encompassing the Mormon church and its view of Joseph Smith that I have chosen to quote it in its entirety. Please take the time to read the following quotation carefully.

> For a hundred years, the early L.D.S. leaders taught us that the Church of Jesus Christ of Latter-day Saints was founded on the rock of revelation. L.D.S. leaders have

148

also taught that the word of God was the iron rod, and that this iron rod was the only sure thing upon which we could safely rely.

We understood that the early leaders of the L.D.S. Church were persecuted and hated among men because they were truly followers of the Lord Jesus Christ. This was in fulfillment of the Lord's teachings, "And ye shall be hated of all men for my name's sake . . ." (Matthew 10:22). We were taught to believe in life eternal and all the rest of the pure teachings of Mormonism which were once beautiful, concrete and scriptural.

We were further taught that the gospel is the same yesterday, today and forever, and that all prophets, sustaining and complementing one another, taught the same, unchanging principles and ordinances. "Adam, Seth, Enoch, Noah, all the Patriarchs and Prophets, Jesus and the Apostles, and every man that has ever written the word of the Lord, have written the same doctrine upon the same subject; and you never can find that Prophets and Apostles clashed in their doctrines in ancient days; neither will they now, if all would at all times be led by the Spirit of salvation"(Brigham Young, *Journal of Discourses*, vol. 5, p. 329).

The scriptures make it clear that if any man were to teach any other doctrine than that formerly taught by the prophets, he would be cursed. "But though we, or an angel from heaven, preach any other gospel unto you than that which we have preached unto you, let him be accursed" (Galatians 1:8) . . . And if any man preach another Gospel than that which I have preached, he shall be cursed . . .(Joseph Smith, *History of the Church*, vol. 6, p. 365).

It is understood that we will be judged by the knowledge we had and the opportunities we had, and more particularly by that which was and is and shall be written. "For behold, out of the books which have been written, and which shall be written, shall this people be judged, for by them shall their works be known unto men. And behold, all things are written by the Father; therefore out of the books written by the Father; therefore out of the books which shall be written shall the world be judged" (*Book of Mormon*, III Nephi 27:25-26; See also Revelation 20:12 in the Bible). Obviously, those things written and designated as scripture are of great importance to us. They will be instrumental in our judgment and will stand as perfectly valid teachings from the Lord. What has happened, and where do we go from here? We are now told that the teachings in the Doctrine and Covenants are not necessarily up to date. They seem to be little more than temporary ideas of a man, subject to correction and change by more enlightened, modern men. Some of the so-called revelations seem to have no present merit, since they are out of harmony with the teachings of our present church leaders, who are apparently more capable of serving the needs of humanity. As a result, an intense "follow the living prophet" campaign has been highly successful and we are now instructed that the iron rod is the word of the living prophet. Following on the heels of this tragedy is the concept that the gospel is as changeable as man may dictate, and that somehow God must comply with man's decisions. Man still attempts to create God in his own image. The living prophet has somehow become empowered to change, twist, turn and annul any and all that has been established as the word of God by all former prophets. The words revealed to them from God suffer change or extinction when the prophets die.

When a prophet dies, his words die with him, or are fair game for change and interpretation, unless his words happen to comply with those of the next living prophet. This is an insecurity not substantiated by scripture. It is true that the living prophet came before scripture, having created the scripture. But no living prophet of any age has the right to annul the word of God that came through a former prophet pertaining to principle and ordinance. They stand forever. Unless his word is now alterable, the Prophet Joseph Smith plainly declared, "Ordinances instituted in the heavens before the foundation of the world, in the priesthood, for the salvation of men, are not to be altered or changed. All must be saved on the same principles (Teachings of the Prophet Joseph Smith, p. 308).

Apparently the Bible, *Book of Mormon*, *Doctrine and Covenants*, and the *Pearl of Great Price* are no longer considered of paramount value, for several prophecies and teachings found in those scriptures are now out of harmony with present church rule. A church spokesman and leader recently said, "The words of the current Mormon president are more important than the teachings of past church leaders, and more vital even than the church's standard written doctrinal works, including the Bible and Book of Mormon" (*Salt Lake Tribune*, Feb 27, 1980 e.). This presents an up to date conflict with the late president of the L.D.S. church, Joseph Fielding Smith, Jr., who said, "If I ever say anything which is contrary to the scriptures, then the scriptures prevail" (Church News, August 23, 1975) It appears that the past living prophet doesn't agree with the present living prophet. The present leader has assumed the right to make null and void many of the words and prophecies of earlier prophets, even though the act of doing so only fulfills them.

What has become of Mormonism? It now changes so fast that a holy principle one day becomes a sin the next. What was formerly the will or word of God is as changeable as the wind, changes made for the advancement of humanity and church members. Yet, every change in Mormon doctrine over the past 100 years has been made to make the church conform more fully to the wishes of the world.

In simple terms, if Christ and His apostles and Joseph Smith and his apostles, had only had the wisdom of the present church leaders, there would never have been the great persecutions of the early Christians or of the early

Mormons. Their gospel remained unchanging, and they suffered the consequences. The word now is to capitulate and placate. Those principles that caused persecutions were actually unnecessary, and we must now apologize for the mistakes of the early prophets and feel shame when their teachings (for which their blood was shed in testimony) are mentioned. The posture now is to shake hands with the world and be one with them. Brigham Young said he dreaded that day.

Have we sold ourselves for the praise of the world? Have we put aside that which was of great value, for that which is of naught? Is the First Presidency of the L.D.S. church now presiding over God? Does Cain now sit in the House of God, claiming he is God? "Let no man deceive you by any means, for that day (the day of Christ) shall not come, except there come a falling away first, and that man of sin be revealed, the son of perdition. Who opposeth and exalteth himself above all that is called God, or that is worshiped; so that he as God sitteth in the temple of God, shewing himself that he is god" (II Thess. 2:3-4).

Urging Mormons to "follow the living prophet" is an invitation to lean upon the arm of flesh, rather than to put our trust in God. This is also contrary to scripture. "Thus saith the Lord; Cursed be the man that trusteth in man, and maketh flesh his arm, and whose heart departeth from the Lord" (Jeremiah 17:5). "The weak things of the world shall come forth and break down the mighty and strong ones, that man should not counsel his fellowman, neither trust in the arm of flesh" (*Doctrine and Covenants*, Sec. 1:19).

Men and women today are called apostates if they believe and uphold that which was formerly taught by church prophets, while those who reject those teachings are called the true Saints! This is a complete reversal of the meaning of the word "Apostate." Apostates depart from revealed truth. But more people are now excommunicated for believing the teachings, all of the teachings, of the founders of Mormonism, than for any other cause.

Isaiah saw our day and prophesied, ". . . But they also have erred through wine, and through strong drink are out of the way; the priest and the prophet have erred through strong drink, they are swallowed up of wine, they are out of the way through strong drink; they err in vision, they stumble in judgment" (Isaiah 28:7). Wine and strong drink suggest pride and power. Further, "As for my people, children are their oppressors, and women rule over them. O my people, they which lead thee cause thee to err, and destroy the way of thy paths" (*Ibid.* 3:12).

Submission of Ephraim to the world was prophesied in these words of Isaiah: "Because ye have said, We have made a covenant with death, and with hell are we at agreement; when the overflowing scourge shall pass through, it shall not come unto us, for we have made lies our refuge, and under falsehood have we hid ourselves" (*Ibid.* 28:15). Nephi records the same words from Isaiah, and includes the statement, "The Lord hath broken the staff of the wicked, the scepters of the rulers" (II Nephi 24:5).

If one holding the scepter of God could lead the people astray in earlier ages, why has it become so unthinkable that the present leaders could lead the people into error? Former leaders thought to change principles and ordinances, and they did. But the people in that long ago day were just as certain that their living leader wouldn't lead them astray. Today, many are also certain that no living prophet could lead anyone into error. It is a peculiarity that the living of all ages claim infallibility for the living, but readily admit to the errors of the dead. But is the president of the L.D.S. church nigh unto God? Or is the Pope of Rome the Vicar of Christ? Oh, you good Mormons, stop trying to think for yourselves! No longer must you know for yourselves, for there is no need. Put your trust in man; cease praying, cease fasting, lest you know the truth and the truth set you free, lest you know the truth and be excommunicated!

"The ancient and honorable, he is the head; and the prophet that teacheth lies, he is the tail, For the leaders of this people cause them to err; and they that are led of them are destroyed" (Isaiah 9:15-16).

So we seem to have modern church leaders quoting the dead leaders when those quotations agree with modern humanism, and we are assured that we never will be led into error. We are told that it is alright for living prophets to institute doctrinal changes, for no living prophet is permitted to err. The idea is unscriptural, as we have noted. Even the Prophet Joseph Smith was given several stern warnings one of which told him to beware lest he fall (*Doctrine and Covenants* 3:9). It was very likely, then, that he could. The scriptures also make provision for the President of the High Priesthood of the L.D.S. church. "And inasmuch as a President of the High Priesthood shall transgress, he shall be had in remembrance before the common council of the church . . . thus, none shall be exempted from the justice and the laws of God . . ." (*Ibid*, 107:81-84). Section 43 of the same scripture, verse 4, states that the prophet can fall and would have no other power save to appoint another in his stead. Section 20, verse 34, warns even the sanctified to beware. Clearly, mortal man, regardless of position or calling, is not infallible.

The L.D.S. Church is being made acceptable to the world. The early leaders did not assume the authority to change teachings and ordinances, but modern leaders are placed above former prophets and scripture. Realistically, the name of the Church of Jesus Christ of Latter-day Saints could well be changed to the Church of the First Presidency, or the Church of the Living Prophet, moving from Mormonism to Humanism.

Church leaders can and have led men astray. King Noah of Book of Mormon fame is an example of a man prop-

154

erly ordained, who went astray. Abinadi opposed him, and went to the flames. But the leader, King Noah, was opposed. What right did John the Baptist have to oppose the church in his day? For that matter, what right did Jesus have to oppose the church?

Mormons agree that the Saints in the Meridian of time changed laws and ordinances and eventually went astray into apostasy. Why can there not be such a thing as apostasy in the changes made today? Is it because we are much more enlightened and are willing to submit to the pressures of the world? Much has been said about pitting dead prophets against the living prophets. No one would have the opportunity to put dead prophets against living prophets if all taught the same gospel restored by Joseph Smith. They tell us to follow the living prophet. If the living prophet had followed his living prophet, there would be no controversy. Present church leaders are changing many precious things of the gospel taught by our former leaders, and dare to say, "Now follow me!" when they have failed to follow their leaders.

There was a day when we were encouraged to study the scriptures. We were encouraged to read the teachings of the prophets. We were urged to know for ourselves whether we were led of God or of man. Now the direction to us is to leave the teachings of the prophets to the interpretations of church leaders. This is but a step away from book-burning. Presently, books are subjected to removal from shelves, or deletion of important and informative passages in the newer editions. And we await changes planned for our scriptures. "For the things which some men esteem to be of great worth, both to the body and soul, others set at naught and trample under their feet . . ." (I Nephi 19:7). "Woe unto them that turn aside the just for a thing of naught and revile against that which is good, and say that it is of no worth . . ." (II Nephi 28:16).

What does a man have to do before his actions result in

155

"Amen to the priesthood of that man?" Turning against the former prophets, instructing us to "forget what they said," and teaching another gospel, is serious. Truly, if, as prophesied in the 85th Section of the D. & C., the Lord Jesus Christ and the Prophet Joseph Smith were to come to us and stand by their words revealed in this last dispensation, they could not avoid voicing opposition to the present church rule, and again be crucified, or at least excommunicated for their teachings.[164]

This lengthy quote, from a Mormon who believes the basic Mormon scriptures, illustrates the great tension going on in the L.D.S. church today. Yes, as a matter of fact they are ashamed of the teachings of Joseph Smith and their other early prophets, as well they should be.

---

[164] Star of Truth Publishing, Joseph L. Jensen, Chairman, P.O. Box 271, West Jordan, Utah 84084.

ASHAMED OF HIS WRITINGS

*But even though we,
or an angel from heaven,
should preach to you
a gospel contrary to that
which we have preached to you,
let him be accursed . . . .*

Galatians 1:8

They are Ashamed of His Writings

The writings of Joseph Smith are a strange mixture of plagiarism, pseudo-Indian archaeology, the Bible, and revelation (many of which happened to get Joseph Smith out of trouble). The parts that can be traced to Joseph Smith have large doses of bragging tossed in for good measure. He claimed to be a translator and reader of unknown languages. He boasted that he had a hot line to God. Later it was claimed of Joseph, not only that he had conversed with God, but that he was, himself, a god.

While we have briefly discussed the *Book of Mormon* earlier in this book, it is not the *Book of Mormon* which brings the greatest embarrassment to the L.D.S.

Although the *Book of Mormon* is filled with stories that have no basis in fact; even though it is totally unreliable as history; in spite of the fact that it is full of errors—it actually presents a fairly standard view of Christianity. The majority of the false doctrines of the Mormon church are not found in the *Book of Mormon*, but stem out of their other writings, the *Doctrine and Covenants* and the *Pearl of Great Price*. It is these writings to which we will now turn our attention.

CHAPTER FIFTEEN

The Doctrine & Covenants

The *Doctrine and Covenants* is a compilation of 138 "revelations" by which the Bible and the *Book of Mormon* have been expanded. It was first published in 1835, but has been enlarged since that time. The vast majority of these revelations are from Joseph Smith, but there are a couple that were given by Brigham Young and one by Joseph Fielding Smith. The book also includes two "Official Declarations" of the church.

It is this book which contains many of the distinctive teachings of Mormonism, including polytheism, men becoming gods, baptism for the dead, celestial marriage, and plural marriages.

The Mormon church should be greatly embarrassed

by the *Doctrine and Covenants* for many reasons. Here are but a few.

ITS ACCURACY

First of all, it claims to be so accurate that it would never need to be changed.

> What I the Lord have spoken, I have spoken, and I excuse not myself; and though the heavens and the earth pass away, my word shall not pass away, but shall all be fulfilled, whether by mine own voice or by the voice of my servants, it is the same. For behold, and lo, the Lord is God, and the Spirit beareth record, and the record is true, and the truth abideth forever and ever. Amen.[165]

With this in mind, why has the *Doctrine and Covenants* been changed over 2,786 times? We are not talking about simply grammatical errors or spelling corrections, but these changes include over twenty clear doctrinal reversals—twenty theological U-turns—twenty fabulous flip-flops. This is not only something to examine, it is certainly something of which a person should be ashamed![166]

ITS CONTRADICTIONS

Second, the *Doctrine and Covenants* contradicts the Bible as well as the *Book of Mormon*. (It even contradicts itself!) The Bible clearly teaches that if anyone comes

---

[165] *Doctrine and Covenants*, 1:38-39.

[166] For a detailed coverage of this matter, see my book, *The Bible and Mormon Scriptures Compared.*

and brings a different message, even if it were an angel from heaven, that message is not from God, and the messenger should be "accursed."[167] This, in and of itself, should disqualify much of Mormon teaching. The official stance of the L.D.S. church, however, is that the Bible is inaccurate and many plain and precious truths have been removed from it. This being their stance, the Bible in their opinion cannot serve as a qualified judge for the Mormon scriptures.[168]

The *Book of Mormon* cannot be discarded as easily, however. The official stance of the L.D.S. is that the *Book of Mormon* is

> . . . the most correct of any book on earth, and the keystone of our religion, and a man would be nearer to God by abiding its precepts, than by any other book.[169]

It is surprising to find that the Bible and *Book of Mormon* often agree against the *Doctrine and Covenants*. The Bible and the *Book of Mormon* teach that a Christian man should have only one wife, the *Doctrine and Covenants* clearly teaches that for a man to reach exaltation in heaven he must have several wives.

The *Book of Mormon* says:

> And now it came to pass that the people of Nephi, under the reign of the second king, began to grow hard in their hearts, and indulge themselves somewhat in wicked practices, such as like unto David of old desiring

---

[167] Galatians 1:8-9

[168] This was not always the stance of Brigham Young who said, "Take up the Bible, compare the religion of the Latter-day Saints with it and see if it will stand the test." (*Journal of Discourses*, Vol. 16, p. 46.)

[169] Joseph Smith , *History of the Church*, 4:461.

many wives and concubines, and also Solomon, his son.[170]

Behold, David and Solomon truly had many wives and concubines, which thing was abominable before me, saith the Lord . . . Wherefore, the Lord God will not suffer that this people shall do like unto them of old . . . For there shall not any man among you have save it be one wife; and concubines he shall have none . . . .[171]

Behold the Lamanites your brethren, whom ye hate because of their filthiness and the cursing which hath come upon their skins, are more righteous than you; for they have not forgotten the commandment of the Lord, which was given unto our fathers—that they should have save it were one wife, and concubines they should have none, and there should not be whoredoms committed among them.[172]

Isn't it surprising to find the very opposite teaching in another "scripture" of the Mormon church? The *Doctrine and Covenants* says,

Verily, thus saith the Lord unto you my servant Joseph, that inasmuch as you have inquired of my hand to know and understand wherein I, the Lord, justified my servants Abraham, Isaac, and Jacob, as also Moses, David and Solomon, my servants, as touching the principle and doctrine of their having many wives and concubines . . . Therefore, prepare thy heart to receive and obey the instructions which I am about to give unto you; for all those who have this law revealed unto them must obey the same. For behold, I reveal unto you a new and everlasting covenant; and if ye abide not that covenant,

---

[170] *Book of Mormon,* Jacob 1:15.
[171] *Ibid.,* Jacob 2:24-27.
[172] *Ibid.,* Jacob 3:5.

then are ye damned; for no one can reject this covenant and be permitted to enter into my glory . . . and he that receiveth a fullness thereof must and shall abide the law, or he shall be damned, saith the Lord God.[173]

Go ye therefore, and do the works of Abraham; enter ye into my law and ye shall be saved. But if ye enter not into my law ye cannot receive the promise of my Father, which he made unto Abraham. God commanded Abraham, and Sarah gave Hagar to Abraham to wife. And why did she do it? Because this was the law; and from Hagar sprang many people. This therefore, was fulfilling, among other things, the promises.[174]

David also received many wives and concubines, and also Solomon and Moses my servants, as also many others of my servants, from the beginning of creation until this time; and in nothing did they sin save in those things which they received not of me. David's wives and concubines were given unto him of me, by the hand of Nathan, my servant, and others of the prophets who had the keys of this power; and in none of these things did he sin against me save in the case of Uriah and his wife . . . .[175]

Which of these revelations are we supposed to believe?[176] Has God changed his mind? Both the Bible and the *Book of Mormon* tell us that God never changes. Are we to believe that after thousands of years God changed his mind and told Joseph to change the doctrine for Him? Or could it be that this was a "convenient

---

[173] *Doctrine and Covenants*, 132:1-6. Emphasis Mine.

[174] *Ibid.*, 32-34.

[175] *Ibid.*, 38-39.

[176] For other information on this subject you might also see the Bible: 1 Timothy 3:2; *Book of Mormon*, Jacob 2:24-27; and *Doctrine and Covenants*, 132.

revelation" to justify a lifestyle that Joseph had already adopted? The overwhelming evidence points to the latter.

Another area in which the *Book of Mormon* and the Bible agree against the *Doctrine and Covenants* is in the belief of monotheism. Simply stated, both the *Book of Mormon* and the Bible clearly teach that there is but one(mono) God(Theos). Interestingly enough on this matter, the *Doctrine and Covenants* contradicts itself.

Isaiah 43:10 says,

> . . . Understand that I am He: before me there was no God formed, neither shall there be after me.

The *Book of Mormon* says,

> "Yea, there is a true and living God." Now Zeezrom said: "Is there more than one God?" And he answered, "No!"[177]

But the *Doctrine and Covenants* teaches both monotheism and polytheism.

> Then shall they be gods, because they have all power, and the angels are subject unto them.[178]

But it also says:

> [He] gave unto them commandments that they should love and serve him, the only living and true God.[179]

And the list goes on. Not only does the *Doctrine and Covenants* disagree when talking about polygamy and

---

[177] *Book of Mormon*, Alma 11:26-29.
[178] *Doctrine and Covenants*, 132:20.
[179] *Ibid.*, 20:19.

polytheism, it portrays God as having a physical body;[180] it suggests a formation of the earth rather than a creation;[181] it distinguishes between a holy ghost and a holy spirit;[182] it teaches that there will be marriage in heaven;[183] and it suggests that the president of the L.D.S. church is the one who holds the keys of salvation.[184]

There can be no doubt that the disagreement between the *Doctrine and Covenants* and the Bible, and especially the *Doctrine and Covenants* and the *Book of Mormon* has caused some skirmishes among the ranks of the L.D.S.

ITS STRANGE TEACHINGS

A third reason to be ashamed of the *Doctrine and Covenants* is found in that it teaches very strange things about the use of tobacco, hot drinks, and meat. Section 89 of the *Doctrine and Covenants* is often referred to as the "Word of Wisdom" and is the source of these strange teachings.

The "Word of Wisdom" proclaims in verse 8 that,

. . . tobacco is not for the body, neither for the belly, and is not good for man, but is an herb for bruises and all sick cattle, to be used with judgment and skill.

I was unaware that tobacco had medicinal purposes. I will relate this to my son, Doug. He is a dairy farmer

---

[180] *Ibid.*, 130:2.
[181] *Ibid.*, 93:33.
[182] *Ibid.*, 131:7, 8.
[183] *Ibid.*, 132.
[184] *Ibid.*, 84:21, 35.

and I'm sure that this knowledge will be useful to him on the farm. All he needs to do is give a good dose of nicotine to cure a cow's mastitis. Those readers who bruise easily might also take note—here is a way to get rid of those unsightly blemishes! (Sorry, I am being a little sarcastic—but can't you see how this would be embarrassing for a Mormon?)

The "Word of Wisdom" also relates the following: strong drinks are not for the belly, but for the washing of your bodies;[185] hot drinks are not for the belly,[186] and meat should be used sparingly in times of winter, cold, or famine.[187] It has been documented that all of these were broken by Joseph Smith, himself.[188]

Although some of the "Words of Wisdom" are stressed by the Mormon church today, most portions are almost completely ignored. Why? Because they are ridiculous and embarrassing to the Mormon church!

---

[185] *Ibid.*, 89:7.

[186] *Ibid.*, 89:9.

[187] *Ibid.*, 89:12, 13.

[188] See Jerald and Sandra Tanner's book, *The Changing World of Mormonism* , p. 469.

CHAPTER SIXTEEN

The Pearl of Great Price

The *Pearl of Great Price* is a document that was first published in 1851. It is usually companioned with the *Doctrine and Covenants* in one volume and contains, "The Book of Moses,"[189] "The Book of Abraham,"[190] "Extracts from the History of Joseph Smith,"[191] and "The Articles of Faith."[192]

---

[189] Eight chapters of the *Inspired Version* of the Bible which was edited by Joseph Smith. These parallel Genesis 1-6.

[190]Smith's 1842 "translation" of an Egyptian papyrus manuscript found with some mummies excavated near Thebes in 1831. It is said to have been written by Abraham himself, but turned out to be one of the greatest embarrassments to the L.D.S. church. It is a proven fraud.

[191] Excerpts from the diary of Joseph Smith.

[192] Propositions summarizing the Mormon faith. First published by Joseph Smith in response to newspaper request.

While much could be said about all of these sections, we will focus our attention on the point of the greatest embarrassment for Mormons today—the *Book of Abraham.*

Joseph Smith claims in the heading to this book that it is,

A Translation of some ancient Records, that have fallen into our hands from the catacombs of Egypt. —The writings of Abraham while he was in Egypt, called the *Book of Abraham*, written by his own hand, upon papyrus.

This is of particular importance because it is the only work of Joseph Smith which we can study in light of the papyrus from which it was translated. In other words, we can actually check the work of Joseph to see if he translated it accurately. With the *Book of Mormon,* we don't have the "golden tablets" to verify Joseph's translation. The *Doctrine and Covenants* consists of "visions" to the prophet. It is hard to use the scientific method on a dream. But we have the manuscripts for the *Book of Abraham* by which we can check the translating skills of Joseph Smith. What are the results of such a study?

The translation of the *Book of Abraham* is a total farce! This papyrus was not a writing by Abraham at all, but was a small Egyptian funeral text of some fifty-seven letters. Joseph took these fifty-seven letters and "translated" them into over 4,400 words. One small Egyptian letter was translated into over seventy words with seven names.

It is embarrassing when Mormons realize the extent to which Joseph Smith was wrong. Egyptologist, Mormon priest, and professor, Dee Jay Nelson was able to examine the materials from which Joseph Smith claimed to translate the *Book of Abraham*. What was the result of his testing? He left the Mormon church and stated,

> The scientific world finds the *Book of Abraham* an insult to intelligence. Some of the most brilliant and qualified Egyptologists of our time have labeled it fraudulent upon the overwhelming evidence of the recently discovered Metropolitan-Joseph Smith Papyri. No truly qualified Egyptologist has yet supported it. We do not wish to be associated with a church which teaches lies and racial bigotry.[194]

The *Book of Abraham* is indeed a scam and is something to be very ashamed about. If there was no other proof of Joseph Smith's dishonesty, this would be enough to convict him in any court of law, and should raise more than doubt in the mind of any reasonable person. We will discuss the *Book of Abraham* further in Chapter 20.

Another embarrassment can be found in the section called "Joseph Smith" in the *Pearl of Great Price*. It is a wholesale condemnation of all other churches as being of the devil.

> My object in going to inquire of the Lord was to know which of all the sects was right, that I might know which to join. No sooner, therefore, did I get possession of myself, so as to be able to speak, than I asked the Personages who stood above me in the light, which of all the sects was right—and which I should join. I was answered that I must join none of them, for they were

---

[194] Dee Jay Nelson, *The Joseph Smith Papyri*, Part 2. Salt Lake City, 1978. See also Tanner, *Mormonism, Shadow or Reality?*, in their chapter "The Fall of the Book of Abraham."

all wrong; and the Personages who addressed me said that all their creeds were an abomination in his sight; that those professors were all corrupt; that: "they draw near to me with their lips, but their hearts are far from me, they teach for doctrines the commandments of men, having a form of godliness, but they deny the power thereof."[195]

What would you think if your religious leader was a liar, sex fiend, brawler, boaster, thief, and yet condemned all religious people as hypocrites? I would be ashamed to associate with such a group and especially their prophet. Is it any wonder that the Mormon church is de-emphasizing the role of their prophet?

Above is a photograph of the right side of the original fragment of papyrus from which Joseph Smith was supposed to have translated the Book of Abraham.

---

[195] Joseph Smith, *Pearl of Great Price*, 2:18-19.

This is a photograph of the original manuscript of the Book of Abraham as it appears in *Joseph Smith Egyptian Alphabet and Grammar.*[196]

---

[196] The photocopies of the original Egyptian papyrus from which Joseph "translated" the *Book of Abraham* are not very clear as they are photos of photos. We apologize for this.

The point we wish to make is clearly discernable from these copies. Joseph took fifty or so Egyptian characters and translated them into over 4,000 words in the *Book of Abraham*.

Look carefully at the Egyptian papyrus photo. Above a letter that looks like a backwards E, is an arrow marked "1." Look at Joseph's handwritten copy. It becomes crystal clear that Joseph could not and did not translate the Egyptian.

One letter is translated into 56 words with seven names. It is impossible for this to be considered (as it is stated in the heading of the *Book of Abraham*) a translation of some Egyptian.

CHAPTER SEVENTEEN

The Inspired Version

Many people do not know that Joseph Smith made his own translation of the Bible. The work is called the *Inspired Version*. This project was started in the spring of 1831[197] and was completed by Joseph on July 2, 1833.[198] In the *Inspired Version*, Joseph made over 4,000 changes in the biblical text—changes which could hardly be called minor. In one instance, Joseph removed an entire Bible book. In another instance, multiple verses (containing over 800 words) were added to substantiate his claims. Joseph greatly expanded the Sermon on the Mount. Joseph altered the Book of Genesis. The Bible

---

[197] *The Restored Church*, 1956, p. 134.
[198] Joseph Smith, *History of the Church*, Vol. 1, p. 368.

was even enlarged by including prophecies which testify that Joseph was a true prophet of God. One of these passages reads:

> A seer shall the Lord my God raise up . . . And that seer will I bless . . . for this promise I give unto you; for I will remember you from generation to generation; and his name shall be called Joseph, and it shall be after the name of his father; and he shall be like unto you; for the thing which the Lord shall bring forth by his hand shall bring my people unto salvation.[199]

Besides adding his own name to the Bible, Joseph used this opportunity to add many of his own heretical views. This is evident when you read his account of Cainan in Genesis. The addition clearly shows his prejudice against Negroes.

> And there was a blackness came upon all the children of Cainan, that they were despised among all people . . . . and it came to pass, that Enoch continued to call upon all the people, save it were the people of Cainan, to repent. . . . and Enoch also beheld the residue of the people which were the sons of Adam, and they were a mixture of all the seed of Adam, save it were the seed of Cain; for the seed of Cain were black, and had not place among them.[200]

The changes in the Bible are so numerous that Joseph Smith's hand must have become weary from writing. Joseph lacked any reverence for the Holy Scriptures and freely propagated the "paste and cut" method of writing. Although his work has often been called a transla-

---

[199] *Inspired Version*, Genesis 50:24-36.
[200] *Ibid.*, Genesis 7:10,14-29.

tion, it was not really a translation at all, but rather a reworking and re-editing of the King James Version of the Bible. Bruce R. McConkie speaks about the *Inspired Version* in his book, *Mormon Doctrine,*

> . . . at the command of the Lord and while acting under the spirit of revelation, the Prophet corrected, revised, altered, added to, and deleted from the King James Version of the Bible to form what is now commonly referred to as the Inspired Version . . . .[201]

Even though the Mormons realize that this document was a work of their prophet, Joseph Smith, and in spite of the fact that he claimed it to be a project ordained by God, the *Inspired Version* has been a source of much embarrassment for Mormon church leaders. The book contains revisions, additions, and deletions which can be shown to be totally unsubstantiated. The writing also contains numerous errors that prove that it could not have been accomplished by the inspiration of God.

One would expect that if Joseph Smith revised the Bible by the inspiration of God, the task would be an easy one. You could easily accomplish it simply by writing down what God had to say. You would also expect that if God was involved, the project would be done in an orderly fashion and that it would be extremely accurate (if not perfect) the first time around. It is surprising to find that Joseph not only revised the Bible, he revised and reworked his own revisions (actually, at this point—there is very little about Joseph Smith that is surprising). Upon Joseph Smith's death, many of the

---

[201] Bruce R. McConkie, *Mormon Doctrine*, 1958, pp. 351-352.

manuscripts of the *Inspired Version* were left in great dis-array and were found to contain numerous errors and blatant contradictions!

> Many texts reveal that the process was not some kind of automatic verbal or visual revelatory experience on the part of Joseph Smith. He often caused a text to be writ-ten in one form and later reworded his initial revision. The manuscripts in some cases show a considerable time lapse between such reconsiderations.[202]

It is easy to see why the Mormons are ashamed of the *Inspired Version*. They are so embarrassed by the revision that the Utah Branch of the Mormon church has never published an official copy of Joseph Smith's work— even though their own scriptures claim that its printing was commanded by God. In talking with two Mormon missionaries today in my office, I questioned them con-cerning the *Inspired Version*—their answer came in typi-cal L.D.S. terminology (actually it sounded rehearsed). "The work of Joseph Smith was never completed and therefore we still use the King James Version of the Bible. We do not use the *Inspired Version*."

But, despite their claims that the work was not fin-ished, the *Inspired Version* was completed by Joseph Smith in 1833. In the *History of the Church,* under the date of February 2, 1833, we find this statement by Joseph Smith: "We this day finished the translating of the Scriptures."[203] Why would the Mormons deny that the version was completed?

---

[202] James R. Harris, Thesis Paper from Brigham Young University, p. 151.

[203] Joseph Smith, *History of the Church,* Vol. 1, p. 368.

Part of the answer is found in the fact that the book was never published during Joseph Smith's own lifetime. After Joseph was killed in prison, his wife Emma was asked by Brigham Young (through a messenger) to turn over the manuscript to him. Emma refused. Later, in 1866, Emma gave the manuscript to the Reorganized Church of Jesus Christ of Latter-day Saints and it was published within the year.

Brigham Young was distraught because the "apostate" branch had published Joseph's translation. In an attempt to downplay the importance of this new manuscript, Brigham Young made some interesting comments. In one statement he suggested that there was no need for a new rendition of the Bible. Brigham Young said that ". . . the Bible is good enough just as it is, it will answer my purpose . . . ."[204] This is an interesting statement in light of the fact that the first "Prophet" of the church said the Bible was full of errors and needed revision. One should also remember that the *Doctrine and Covenants* contains at least eighteen sections where Joseph Smith is instructed to complete and publish the revision. Did Brigham Young doubt the revelations of God that were given to Joseph Smith in the *Doctrine and Covenants*? Why hasn't the Mormon church followed through with the commandments of God?

The following passages make it quite clear that Joseph Smith was commanded to print and publish the *Inspired Version*.

> . . . I have commanded you to organize, even to shinelah (to print) my words, the fullness of my scriptures.[205]

---

[204] Brigham Young, *Journal of Discourses*, Vol. 3, p. 116.
[205] *Doctrine and Covenants*, 104:58.

And again he was told to,

> ... publish the new translation of my holy word unto the inhabitants of the earth.[206]

But Brigham Young and others have been opposed to the *Inspired Version*. Brigham took great pains to make sure that this document did not fall into the hands of any of his people. Orson Pratt, however, was in disagreement with Brigham Young on this issue and felt that this work was of great value. Many Mormon authors have taken sides with Orson and frequently use the *Inspired Version* in their teaching. But the Mormon church has not printed these "scriptures."

Before Joseph Fielding Smith became president of the church, he pushed for the printing of the *Inspired Version*. But when he became president in 1970, the church still took no steps towards fulfilling the commands of God. Why? It is simply because they are embarrassed by it.

The Tanners, in their book, *The Changing World of Mormonism*, speak to this issue:

> We do not feel . . . that any president will allow this book to be printed because it would tend to embarrass the church and to show that Joseph Smith was not a prophet of God.
>
> The Mormon church is faced with a peculiar dilemma with regard to Joseph Smith's "inspired revision." They cannot reject it entirely without admitting that he was a deceiver. On the other hand, if they were to print the

---

[206] *Doctrine and Covenants*, 124:89.

revision and fully endorse it, they would be faced with equally unsurmountable problems. The contents of the "inspired revision" actually contradict doctrines that are now taught in the Mormon church. Therefore, the Mormon church can neither fully accept nor fully reject the Inspired Version of the Bible.[207]

Today we have enough manuscript evidence to know for certain that our current Bible is extremely accurate. We can check our Bibles against the original text of the scriptures. The results of such a test show that our Bibles are accurate, and that Joseph Smith's rendition is an attempt to tamper with what can be documented to be the Word of God. We know for certain that Joseph Smith was mistaken when he said,

> I believe the Bible as it read when it came from the pen of the original writers. Ignorant translators, careless transcribers, or designing and corrupt priests have committed many errors.[208]

Even the *Book of Mormon* claims that the Bible has been tampered with and changed.

> And after they go forth by the hands of the twelve apostles of the Lamb, from the Jews unto the Gentiles, thou seest the foundation of a great and abominable church, which is most abominable above all other churches; for behold they have taken away from the gospel of the Lamb many parts which are plain and most precious; and also many covenants of the Lord have they taken away.[209]

---

[207] *The Changing World of Mormonism*, p. 385.
[208] *History of the Church*, Vol. 6, p. 57.
[209] *Book of Mormon*, 1 Nephi 13:26.

Again Nephi is made to say:

> Wherefore, thou seest that after the book hath gone forth through the hands of the great and abominable church, that there are many plain and precious things taken away from the book, which is the book of the Lamb of God.[210]

Joseph Smith is the one who has schemed to corrupt the Bible. Joseph is the one who made over 4,000 changes in the biblical text in his "translation." Joseph has not improved on the Bible, but has given us a certifiable corruption of it. It is no wonder that the Utah Branch of the Mormon movement claims that "it was not completed and we will not publish it."

The work of Joseph Smith brings to mind a few passages in the Bible. The first can be found in Galatians.

> I am amazed that you are so quickly deserting Him who called you by the grace of Christ, for a different gospel; which is really not another; only there are some who are disturbing you, and want to distort the gospel of Christ. But even though we, or an angel from heaven, should preach to you a gospel contrary to that which we have preached to you, let him be accursed.[211]

The second passage might be even more appropriate:

> I testify to everyone who hears the words of the prophecy of this book: if anyone adds to them, God shall add to him the plagues which are written in this book; and if anyone takes away from the words of the book of this prophecy, God shall take away his part from the tree of life and from the holy city, which are written in this

---

[210] *Ibid.*, 1 Nephi 13:28
[211] Galatians 1:6-8

book. He who testifies to these things says, "Yes, I am coming quickly." Amen. Come, Lord Jesus.[212]

Finally,

But realize this, that in the last days difficult times will come. For men will be lovers of self, lovers of money, boastful, arrogant, revilers . . . unholy . . . without self control, brutal . . . conceited, lovers of pleasure rather than lovers of God; holding to a form of godliness, although they have denied its power; and avoid such men as these. For among them are those who enter into households and captivate weak women weighed down with sins, led on by various impulses, always learning and never able to come to the knowledge of the truth.[213]

The Bible is right. Everyone who claims to be a prophet of God isn't necessarily what they claim. Joseph has been found guilty of changing the very Word of God, taking away and adding to it. He certainly rests under God's curse.

Timothy's words are almost biographical of Joseph. He was a lover of self, money; was arrogant, unholy and conceited. He had a form of godliness—but has been found to be a womanizer who gave himself over to lusts and pleasure. Because of his hard heart and sin, Joseph never did come close to discovering the truth.

---

[212] Revelation 22:18-20
[213] 2 Timothy 3:1-7

ASHAMED OF HIS TRUE HISTORY

You don't know me:
you never knew my heart.
No man knows my history.
I cannot tell it;
I shall never undertake it.
I don't blame anyone
for not believing my history.

Joseph Smith

CHAPTER EIGHTEEN

Ashamed of His Mother's History

Few people know a person better than their mother. Mothers see the best in their children and have a tendency to remember every good thing and often forget those things that are an embarrassment. We all need our mothers.

If Joseph's mother's history of him would be in error it would be, most likely, in over-glorifying him. (Wouldn't it be wonderful if we had an account of the life of Jesus as written by his mother, Mary? If we did we could certainly expect it to be honest and forthright).

We do have a history of Joseph Smith written by his mother. She claims this writing to be very accurate:

Here ends the history of my life, as well as that of my family, as far as I intend carrying it for the present. And

I shall leave the world to judge, as seemeth them good, concerning what I have written. But this much I will say, that the testimony which I have given is true, and will stand forever; and the same will be my testimony in the day of God Almighty, when I shall meet them, concerning whom I have testified, before angels, and spirits of the just made perfect, before archangels and seraphims, cherubims and gods; where the brief authority of the unjust man will shrink to nothingness before him who is the Lord of lords, and God of gods; and where righteousness of the just shall exalt them in the scale, wherein God weigheth the hearts of men. And now having, in common with the Saints, appealed in vain for justice, to Wilburn W. Boggs, Thomas Carlin, Martin Van Buren and Thomas Ford, I bid them a last farewell, until I shall appear with them before Him who is the judge of both the quick and dead; to whom I solemnly appeal in the name of Jesus Christ. Amen.[214]

The L.D.S. church has found this biography very embarrassing to them and have changed it significantly in spite of the sworn oath before Jesus Christ by his mother that it was accurate.

If Joseph Smith was, as he stated, greater than any other person who ever lived, including Jesus Christ, this history should prove Joseph Smith a true prophet.

The book is entitled, *History of Joseph Smith by His Mother Lucy Mack Smith*. It might better be named, "A History of Lucy Mack Smith with Comments on Joseph." A lot is said about the writer, almost as much if not more than is said about the prophet.

She had finished her book by October of 1845 and wanted the church to print it.[215] The book was finally

---

[214] Lucy Mack Smith, *History of Joseph Smith*, pp. 327-328.
[215] *Times and Seasons*, Vol. 6, p. 1014.

printed in 1853 by the Apostle Orson Pratt under the title *Biographical Sketches of Joseph Smith Prophet, and His Progenitors for Many Generations.*

At first this book was recommended reading. The *Deseret News* recommended that this book,

> Should be possessed by all saints who feel in the least degree interested with the history of the latter day work.[216]

By the year 1865, however, Brigham Young told members of the Mormon church that he wanted Lucy Smith's history to be suppressed. In the Latter-day Saints' *Millennial Star* for October 21, 1865, Lucy Smith's history was severely condemned by the First Presidency of the church.

Brigham Young said:

> Happening lately, while on a preaching trip . . . to pick up a book which was lying on a table . . . we were surprised to find that it was the book . . . by Lucy Smith . . . Our surprise at finding a copy of this work may be accounted for, by the fact of our having advertised some time ago that the book was incorrect, and that it should be gathered up and destroyed, so that no copies should be left . . . In Great Britain diligence has been used in collecting and in disposing of this work, and we wish that same diligence continued there and also exercised here, at home, until not a copy is left . . . We could go through the book and point out many false statements . . . but we do not feel to do so. It is sufficient to say that it is utterly unreliable as a history, as it contains many falsehoods and mistakes . . . we, therefore expect . . . every one in the church, male and female, if they have such a book, to dispose of it so that it will never be read by any

---

[216] *Deseret News*, Nov. 16, 1854.

person again . . . those who have been instructed respecting its character, and will still keep it on their tables, and have it in their houses as a valid and authentic history for their children to read, need rebuke. It is transmitting lies to posterity to take such a course, and we know that the curse of God will rest upon every one, after he comes to the knowledge of what is here said who keeps these books for his children to learn and believe lies.[217]

It appears that the Apostle Orson Pratt had made a very serious mistake by publishing Joseph's mother's history of him. It is strange that an "Apostle" did not have better judgment.

Therefore the Mormon leaders decided to revise the book. Joseph F. Smith said:

. . . it was disapproved by President Young on August 23, 1865, and the edition was suppressed or destroyed. While some statements contained in the work were considered somewhat overdrawn . . . its many merits were fully recognized by the authorities, many of whom were greatly disappointed at the necessity of issuing the order to temporarily suppress its further circulation.

Subsequently, a committee of revision was appointed by President Young consisting of President George A. Smith and Judge Elias Smith, cousins of the Prophet, men personally familiar with the family and thoroughly conversant with Church history. They were instructed carefully to revise and correct the original work throughout, which they did, reporting their labors to President Young to his entire satisfaction. The revised and only authentic copy thus prepared and reported upon was retained by President George A. Smith, and shortly after his death, September 1, 1875, it was com-

---

[217] *Millennial Star*, Vol. 27, pp. 657-658.

mitted into my keeping, where it has remained until now.[218]

The sad thing about this revision is that Brigham Young did not ask them to put in footnotes where the changes were made, as any honest historian should do. Actual changes were made in the text and the public is not informed, leaving doubt as to what is authentic and what is not.

This disturbing process of changing original documents without any kind of notice has been practiced with most all important Mormon documents including the *Book of Mormon, Doctrine and Covenants* and the *Pearl of Great Price*, leaving most uncertain what was originally given by the prophet.

In preparation for this chapter, I tried earnestly to find a copy of the original work, but was unable to do so. We are left therefore to quote from a work done by Jerald and Sandra Tanner.

> In comparing the first edition of Lucy Smith's history— i.e., the edition Brigham Young tried to destroy—with the edition printed in 1954, we have found that 436 words have been added, 1,379 words deleted and 220 words have been changed. This is a total of 2,035 words added, deleted or changed without any indication. In addition, 736 words have been deleted with the omissions properly indicated.
>
> On page 225 of the first edition of Lucy Smith's book we find the following:

---

[218] Joseph F. Smith, *History of Joseph Smith, by His Mother Lucy Mack Smith*, 1901 edition, Introduction, pp. VII, VIII.

"Here I shall introduce a brief history of our troubles in Missouri, given by my son Hyrum, before the Municipal Court, at Nauvoo, June 30, 1843, when Joseph was tried for treason against the State of Missouri:"

On page 225 of the second edition of Lucy Smith's book we find the following:

"Here I shall introduce a brief history of our troubles in Missouri, given by my son Hyrum, before the Municipal Court, at Nauvoo, June 30, 1843, when Joseph was before the Municipal Court, at Nauvoo, June 30, 1843, on a writ of habeas corpus:"[219]

There is a little bit of discrepancy here. The original text indicates that Joseph was brought up on charges of treason while the edited version indicates that it was a writ of *habeas corpus*. For those of you who are unfamiliar with the implications of these charges—treason is,

The offense of attempting by overt acts to overthrow the government of the state to which the offender owes allegiance or to kill or personally injure the sovereign or his family.[220]

While *habeas corpus* carries an entirely different meaning;

any of several common-law writs issued to bring a party before a court or judge.[221]

---

[219] Jerald & Sandra Tanner, *Mormonism, Shadow or Reality?*
[220] *Webster's New Collegiate Dictionary, 150th Anniversary Edition.*
[221] *Ibid.*

There is quite a bit of difference between these two. The event to which Lucy referred to, was in fact, treason. Joseph had raised up an army to defy the State of Illinois. He had made boasts about what he was going to do to the governor. Lucy's account was the accurate one; the changed version has had the Madison Avenue treatment and gives a very false view of the *actual* facts.

It is dishonest to try to rewrite history to comply with what we wished had happened rather than what actually happened. In my opinion, to cover up the truth is no different than to lie. This problem is a serious one. Should a group of people be allowed to use scissors and paste to edit a historical document? Yet, it has inappropriately been done.

Biblical documents have been carefully checked with the very oldest manuscripts and corrected to reflect what was originally written. But just the opposite has been done in these writings. A modern view has been inserted to cushion the blow of the true historical account.

Why would a religion be ashamed of the account given by the Prophet's own mother? Because the credibility of Joseph Smith has needed a Madison Avenue refashioning by modern writers, to cover up what he was. They are ashamed, as well they should be, of the real Joseph Smith.

The fact of the matter is, however, that even the changed edition should be an embarrassment to the Latter-day Saints. Let us take a brief look at some of its contents.

CHAPTER NINETEEN

A History of Superstition

Since we do not have a copy of the original we will quote from the present edition, *History of Joseph Smith, by His Mother*. The book is filled with the occult, the cabal, mystical, superstitious and fallacious. This sort of thing begins in the family long before Joseph Smith took up these practices. His mother and father repeatedly had spiritual or occult experiences that seem more fitting for a spiritualist medium than a godly family.

MIRACULOUS RECOVERIES

Here are a few examples: Lovisa, Lucy's sister, became ill and miraculously recovered.

As before stated, after the space of two years she began to manifest signs of convalescence, but soon a violent re-attack brought her down again, and she grew worse and worse until she became entirely speechless, and so reduced that her attendants were not allowed to even turn her in bed. She took no nourishment except a very little rice water. She lay in this situation three days and two nights. On the third night, about two o'clock, she feebly pronounced the name of Lovina, (her sister) who had all the while watched over her pillow like an attendant angel, observing every change and symptom with the deepest emotion. Startled at hearing the sound of Lovisa's voice, Lovina now bent over the emaciated form of her sister with thrilling interest, and said, "my sister! my sister! what will you?"

Lovisa then said emphatically, "the Lord has healed me, both soul and body—raise me up and give me my clothes, I wish to get up."

Her husband told those who were watching with her to gratify her, as in all probability it was a revival before death and he would not have her crossed in her last moments.

They did so, though with reluctance, as they supposed she might live a few moments longer if she did not exhaust her strength too much by exerting herself in this manner.

Having raised her in bed, they assisted her to dress; and although, when they raised her to her feet her weight dislocated both of her ankles, she would not consent to return to her bed, but insisted upon being set in a chair and having her feet drawn gently in order to have her ankle joints replaced. She then requested her husband to bring her some wine, saying if he would do so she would do quite well for the present . . . .[222]

---

[222] *History of Joseph Smith, by His Mother, Lucy Mack Smith,* pp. 13-14.

Most Christians believe in answered prayer and healing. I am asking that you not consider just one account but the accounts as a general attitude that began many years before Joseph Smith was even born and these practices continued after his death. Each of these accounts has a part that is absurd or indicate an strong belief in the supernatural as a normal part of every day life. Notice what happened to her ankles. If healed, why did she need additional help? Joseph was raised in this environment.

Again, Lucy tells about an illness that came upon her:

We had lived in Randolph but six months when I took a heavy cold, which caused a severe cough . . . A hectic fever set in which threatened to prove fatal, and the physician pronounced my case to be confirmed consumption . . . I continued to grow weaker and weaker until I could scarcely endure even a foot-fall upon the floor, except in stocking-foot, and no one was allowed to speak in the room above a whisper.

While I was in this situation, a Methodist exhorter came to see me. On coming to the door, he knocked in his usual manner, and his knocking so agitated me that it was a considerable length of time before my nerves became altogether quieted again . . . he showed a great desire to have conversation with me respecting my dying.

. . . I thought I strained my eyes and by doing so I could discern a faint glimmer of the light that was beyond the gloom which lay immediately before me.

. . . I then looked to the Lord and begged and pleaded with him to spare my life in order that I might bring up my children and be a comfort to my husband. My mind was much agitated during the whole night. Sometimes I contemplated heaven and heavenly things, then my thoughts would turn upon those of earth—my babes and my companion.

During the night I made a solemn covenant with God that if He would let me live I would endeavor to serve him according to the best of my abilities. Shortly after this I heard a voice say to me, "Seek, and ye shall find; knock, and it shall be opened unto you. Let your heart be comforted; ye believe in God, believe also in me."

In a few moments my mother came in and, looking upon me, she said, "Lucy, you are better."

I replied, as my speech returned just at that instant, "Yes, mother, the Lord will let me live, if I am faithful to the promise which I made to him, to be a comfort to my mother, my husband, and my children.[223]

This illustrates that Lucy felt that God personally spoke to her and made covenants with her. This was many years before the time when her son claims the same intimate relationship with God. At this point Lucy had not given her life to Christ, become a Christian, or become a part of any church.

VISIONS FROM GOD

Lucy gives an account of her going into the woods to pray and God spoke to her in a dream in answer to her prayer.

While we were living in the town of Tunbridge, my mind became deeply impressed with the subject of religion, which probably was occasioned by my singular experi-

---

[223] *Ibid.*, pp. 33-34.

ence during my sickness at Randolph . . . I retired to a grove not far distant, where I prayed to the Lord in behalf of my husband —that the true gospel might be presented to him and that his heart might be softened so as to receive it, or, that he might become more religiously inclined. After praying some time in this manner, I returned to the house much depressed in spirit, which state of feeling continued until I retired to my bed. I soon fell asleep and had the following dream: I thought that I stood in a large and beautiful meadow, which lay a short distance from the house in which we lived, and that everything around me wore an aspect of peculiar pleasantness. The first thing that attracted my special attention in this magnificent meadow, was a very pure and clear stream of water, which ran through the midst of it; and as I traced this stream, I discovered two trees standing upon its margin, both of which were of the same side of the stream . . . I gazed upon them with wonder and admiration; and after beholding them a short time, I saw one of them was surrounded with a bright belt, that shone like burnished gold, but far more brilliantly. Presently a gentle breeze passed by, and the tree encircled with this golden zone, bent gracefully before the wind, and waved its beautiful branches in the light air. As the wind increased, this tree assumed the most lively and animated appearance, and seemed to express in its motions the utmost joy and happiness. If it had been an intelligent creature, it could not have conveyed, by the power of language, the idea of joy and gratitude so perfectly as it did; and even the stream that rolled beneath it, shared, apparently, every sensation felt by the tree, for, as the branches danced over the stream, it would swell gently, then recede again with a motion as soft as dancing of a sunbeam. The belt also partook of the same influence, and, as it moved in unison with the motion of the stream and of the tree, it increased continually in refulgence and magnitude, until it became exceedingly glorious.

I turned my eyes upon its fellow, which stood opposite; but it was not surrounded with the belt of light as the former, and it stood erect and fixed as a pillar of marble.

No matter how strong the wind blew over it, not a leaf was stirred, not a bough was bent; but obstinately stiff it stood, scorning alike the zephyr's breath, or the power of the mighty storm.

I wondered at what I saw, and said in my heart, What can be the meaning of all this? And the interpretation given me was, that these personated my husband and his oldest brother, Jesse Smith; that the stubborn and unyielding tree was like Jesse; that the other, more pliant and flexible was like Joseph, my husband; that the breath of heaven, which passed over them, was the pure and undefiled gospel of the Son of God, which gospel Jesse would always resist . . . .[224]

Like her son later, Lucy was going into the woods and praying and having personal revelations from God in answer to her prayers. We should not be surprised that her son Joseph would do similarly later.

CHOSEN BY GOD

Lucy recounts another vision that her husband received just shortly after her dream. This fanciful dream confirmed to Joseph Smith Senior that he was also chosen by God along with his family to have God's special blessing.[225]

Dreams as a special revelation of God were a part of family life long before Joseph Smith, the son, claimed such to be his regular experiences.

Lucy had a special revelation from God during her daughter Sophronia's illness in which she knew she would recover from her illness.[226]

---

[224] *Ibid.*, pp. 43-45.
[225] *Ibid.*, pp. 48-50.
[226] *Ibid.*, p. 52.

Her son Joseph (to be the prophet later) was healed from typhus fever that attacked his leg. He not only survived but showed great spirit in enduring the pain of surgery without anesthetic.[227]

She tells of another dream that her husband had:

> I dreamed, that I was traveling on foot, and I was very sick, and so lame I could hardly walk. My guide, as usual, attended me. Traveling some time together, I became so lame that I thought I could go no farther. I informed my guide of this and asked him what I should do. He told me to travel on till I came to a certain garden. So I arose and started for this garden. While on my way thither, I asked my guide how I should know the place. He said, "Proceed until you come to a very large gate; open this and you will see a garden, blooming with the most beautiful flowers that your eyes ever beheld, and there you shall be healed." By limping along with great difficulty, I finally reached the gate; and, on entering it, I saw the before-mentioned garden, which was beautiful beyond description, being filled with the most delicate flowers of every kind and color. In the garden were walks about three and a half feet wide, which were set on both sides with marble stones. One of the walks ran from the gate through the center of the garden; and on each side of this was a very richly carved seat, and on each seat were placed six wooden images, each of which was the size of a very large man. When I came to the first image on the right side, it arose and bowed to me with much deference. I then turned to the one which sat opposite me, on the left side, and it arose and bowed to me in the same manner as the first. I continued turning, first to the right and then to the left, until the whole twelve had made their obeisance, after which I was entirely healed. I then asked my guide the meaning of all this, but I awoke before I received an answer.[228]

---

[227] *Ibid.*, pp. 54-58.
[228] *Ibid.*, pp. 64-65.

The whole history of the family is filled with supernatural events that surpass those of Abraham, Moses, or even of the birth of Jesus.

Am I questioning Lucy's word? Possibly, but more particularly raising the question of whether these events were brought about by God or other powers, if in truth they really happened at all.

WRITING ON BEHALF OF GOD

There is a pattern here that develops long before Joseph Smith's supposed first vision. In Joseph Smith Senior's seventh vision he even thought to ask God to write down instructions for him.

> I dreamed . . . that a man with a peddler's budget on his back, came in and thus addressed me: "Sir, will you trade with me today? I have traded with you each time, and have always found you strictly honest in all your dealings. Your measures are always heaped and your weights over-balance; and I have now come to tell you that this is the last time I shall ever call on you, and that there is but one thing which you lack in order to secure your salvation." As I earnestly desired to know what it was I still lacked, I requested him to write the same upon paper. He said he would do so. I then sprang to get some paper, but in my excitement, I awoke.[229]

Each of these accounts could be critiqued. For example, why would God appear in a dream to tell him something, agree to write it down and then let him awake without doing as He had promised? Why would

---

[229] *Ibid.*, p. 68.

he come to him and then not deliver the message at all? But my purpose is not to critique each account. The quotations are to illustrate that the Smith family, long before Joseph Smith's "First Vision," had been heavily involved in the mystical.

DIVINATION

At this point, in Lucy's biography Joseph Smith Junior comes into the picture with the events surrounding the "First Vision." Since this material is dealt with at another point in this book let us proceed to further evidences of the supernatural.

After Joseph had purportedly received the gold plates, many people are said by Lucy to have sought to obtain them, including several mobs.

Let us take up her story:

> In a short time Joseph received another intimation of the approach of a mob, also of the necessity of removing the Record and breast-plate from the place wherein they were secreted, consequently he took them out of the box in which they were placed, and wrapping them in clothes, carried them across the road to a cooper's shop and laid them in a quantity of flax which was stowed in the shop loft. After which he nailed up the box again, then tore up the floor of the shop and put it under the same.

> As soon as night came, the mob came also and commenced ransacking the place. They rummaged round the house and all over the premises, but did not come into the house. After making satisfactory search, they went away.

> The next morning we found the floor of the cooper's

shop torn up and the box which was laid under it shivered in pieces.

> In a few days afterwards we learned the cause of this last move—why their curiosity led them in the direction of the cooper's shop. A young woman by the name of Chase, sister to Willard Chase, found a green glass through which she could see many very wonderful things, and among her great discoveries she said that she saw the precise place where "Joe Smith kept his gold Bible hid," and obedient to her directions, the mob gathered their forces and laid siege to the cooper's shop.[230]

So, not only is Joseph Smith able to find buried things with his divine looking glass, but Miss Chase is able to divine hidden things as well.[231]

This account is more occult than Christian and appears to be divination rather than the work of God. Yet, it is consistent with the whole of Lucy's biography of her son Joseph.

Martin Harris was a collaborator with Joseph Smith in the production of the *Book of Mormon*. His wife was not sold on the whole story and produced considerable opposition, including trying to find the place where the gold plates were hidden.

On one such occasion she came to the Smiths' home. Let's hear Lucy tell it in her own words:

> As soon as she arrived there, she informed him that her object in coming, was to see the plates, and that she

---

[230] *Ibid.*, p. 113.

[231] If they "shivered" the box in which the gold plates had been hidden, why did they not continue to look for the gold plates?

would never leave until she had accomplished it. Accordingly, without delay, she commenced ransacking every nook and corner about the house—chests, trunks, cupboards, etc.; consequently, Joseph was under the necessity of removing both the breast-plate and the Record from the house, and secreting them elsewhere. Not finding them in the house, she concluded that Joseph had buried them, and the next day she commenced searching out of doors, which she continued to do until about two o'clock p.m. She then came in rather ill-natured; after warming herself a little, she asked Joseph's wife if there were snakes in that country in the winter. She replied in the negative. Mrs. Harris then said, "I have been walking round in the woods to look at the situation of your place, and as I turned round to come home, a tremendous black snake stuck up his head before me, and commenced hissing at me."[232]

The story contains the absurd and the occult. Can you imagine having a guest come to your house and them digging through all of your chests, trunks, cupboards, etc.? If someone did, you would ask them to quit or leave.

It is well known that snakes hibernate in cold weather and especially in northern New York. The obvious intent òf Lucy recounting the story is to impress the reader that a great snake was protecting the gold Bible.

Of course this leads us to the thought that the serpent's biblical import is not godly but satanic. If in fact a snake hissed at Mrs. Harris it seems that the significance of this account is to tie it in with the occult, not Christian system.

These accounts represent but a few of the repeated stories of the mystical, occult, or supernatural that run

---

[232] *Ibid.*, p. 121.

from beginning to end throughout Lucy's work. If in fact the stories are true then the Smith family had more evidences presented to them of their connection with God than any other prophet of God as contained in the Holy Bible.

But, when looked at side by side, it appears that if these events are true history then the source of these mystical happenings is not God but Satan. They bear more similarity to witchcraft than the Holy Spirit of God.

CHAPTER TWENTY

The Embarrassment
of an Egyptian Papyrus

Lucy brings up the subject of the Egyptian Facsimile
that Joseph Smith possessed. Joseph purchased some
old Egyptian papyrus documents from traveling Egyptologists that came through New York. These documents were of interest to him because of his professed
ability to translate ancient documents that others could
not read. This may have been the reason for his mother's reference to "Reformed Egyptian." Notice her statement:

Not long after the circumstance of the mob's going into
the cooper's shop, and splitting in pieces the box,
Joseph began to make arrangements to accomplish the
translation of the Record. The first step that he was
instructed to take in regard to this work was to make a
facsimile of some of the characters, which were called

reformed Egyptian, and to send them to some of the most learned men of this generation and ask them for the translation thereof.[233]

Joseph's ability with "Reformed Egyptian" has been one of his greatest embarrassments. At the time Joseph was looking for "learned men" to look at it, no person on earth could read Egyptian. It was an unreadable language. It was some years later that the Rosetta Stone was found with three languages on it, one of which was Egyptian. At this point Egyptian could then be deciphered.

Although we do not have a copy of the "Reformed Egyptian" of the *Book of Mormon*, spoken of by Lucy, we do have a copy of Joseph's "Reformed Egyptian" of the *Book of Abraham* in the *Pearl of Great Price*.

Since ancient Egyptian can now be read, it is an easy task to check Joseph's ability as a translator. Let me quote from another of my writings.

> The *Book of Abraham* begins with a few comments in the heading above the text which says, "A Translation of some ancient Records, that have fallen into our hands from the catacombs of Egypt,—The writings of Abraham while he was in Egypt, called the Book of Abraham, written by his own hand, upon papyrus." (*Pearl of Great Price*, preface to the *Book of Abraham*).
>
> This would be fantastic information, if it were true. Can you imagine having the very own handwriting of Father Abraham? It would be the only instance of an original handwritten document of any Bible writer. We are immediately skeptical, since Abraham lived so long ago and we do not have any other Bible author's original manuscript.

---

[233] *Ibid.*, p. 114.

Several things make one skeptical about it being possible for such a document to exist. First, papyrus is durable, but not durable enough that it could last for nearly four thousand years in an alligator skin, which is where the archaeologists who sold the manuscript to Joseph Smith are said to have found it. Yet this is the claim that Joseph made for the document.

When Joseph Smith translated the document into the *Book of Abraham* he made a handwritten copy. He placed the "Reformed Egyptian" character in the left hand column and then explained what it meant on the right side of the paper. For years this handwritten copy has been available by photo reprint, but the original Egyptian papyrus was lost. It was supposedly destroyed by the great Chicago fire of 1871.

In 1967 the papyrus was found and presented to the Latter-day Saints Church by the Metropolitan Museum of Art of New York. Thinking that Joseph Smith couldn't possibly have made a mistake, or lied, the church allowed it to be photographed and published in *Dialogue Magazine*. The cat was out of the bag, for this photo copy was submitted to three different Egyptologists for them to independently translate. Each translated it into about seventy words, each with almost identical meanings, each agreeing that it was a quite common type of document that had to do with funerals in Egypt.

Joseph Smith came nowhere close to the meaning that it really had, when he wrote his *Book of Abraham*. In fact, Joseph Smith made it into over four thousand words. This means some characters had to be translated into seventy-five to one hundred or more words, and this from just one Egyptian letter.

We must conclude that Joseph Smith couldn't translate a foreign document. After many years we now have proof that Joseph Smith was a fraud. We do not have the gold plates, but if there were gold plates, and Joseph Smith did seek to translate them, you can be sure he made a mess of it.[234]

Can't you hear the Mormon apologists saying, "Oops, sure wish Lucy had not brought up the subject of 'Reformed Egyptian.' Joseph was found to have lied about that. Yes, we are ashamed."

---

[234] Charles Crane, *The Bible and Mormon Scriptures Compared*, pp. 58-59.

CHAPTER TWENTY-ONE

The Embarrassment of the Gold Plates

For many years those critical of Mormonism have asked to see the gold plates. This should not seem an unreasonable request since this was the same request made by the early witnesses to the *Book of Mormon*.

Even though the *Book of Mormon* has listed the three witnesses and the eight witnesses in the opening pages, these witnesses later all qualified their statements in such a way as to show that none of them really saw the gold plates.

The three witnesses were Oliver Cowdery, age 22, David Whitmer, age 24, and Martin Harris, age 46. Other authors have given full discussion concerning the character of these witnesses. It is not the intention of this work to discuss this in detail, as this book is about Joseph Smith. It does seem wise to give the gist of what can be learned of the reliability of the men who were the primary witnesses.

Jerald and Sandra Tanner say,

> The three witnesses were finally excommunicated from the church. Martin Harris accused Joseph Smith of "lying and licentiousness." The Mormon leaders in turn published an attack on the character of Martin Harris. The *Elders' Journal*—a Mormon publication edited by Joseph Smith—said that Harris and others are guilty of "swearing, lying, cheating, swindling, drinking, with every species of debauchery . . . ." *Elders' Journal,* August, 1838, p. 59.[235]

> In a letter dated December 16, 1838, Joseph Smith said that "John Whitmer, David Whitmer, Oliver Cowdery, and Martin Harris are too mean to mention."[236]

Martin Harris changed his religion thirteen times, eight of which were after he supposedly saw the gold plates of the *Book of Mormon.*

The *Book of Mormon* witnesses were men of very questionable characters, later found involved in all kinds of evil including counterfeiting money.

But back to the main story of Lucy's account of Joseph and the gold Bible—Joseph now had the plates and his enemies were trying to get them from him.

> Joseph kept the Urim and Thummim constantly about his person, by the use of which he could in a moment

---

[235] Jerald and Sandra Tanner, *The Changing World of Mormonism,* p. 96.
[236] *Ibid.,* p. 97.

tell whether the plates were in any danger. Just before Emma rode up to Mr. Wells', Joseph, from an impression that he had, came up out of the well in which he was laboring and met her not far from the house. Emma immediately informed him of what had transpired, whereupon he looked in the Urim and Thummim and saw that the Record was as yet safe; nevertheless, he concluded to return with his wife as something might take place that would render it necessary for him to be at home where he could take care of it . . .

On arriving at home he found his father pacing the ground near his door in great anxiety of mind. Joseph spoke to him, saying, 'Father, there is no danger—all is perfectly safe—there is no cause of alarm . . .

The plates were secreted about three miles from home, in the following manner: Finding an old birch log much decayed, excepting the bark, which was in a measure sound, he took his pocket knife and cut the bark with some care, then turned it back and made a hole of sufficient size to receive the plates, and, laying them in the cavity thus formed, he replaced the bark; after which he laid across the log, in several places, some old stuff that happened to lay near, in order to conceal as much as possible the place in which they were deposited.

Joseph, on coming to them, took them from their secret place, and, wrapping them in his linen frock, placed them under his arm and started for home.

After proceeding a short distance, he thought it would be more safe to leave the road and go through the woods. Traveling some distance after he left the road, he came to a large windfall, and as he was jumping over a log, a man sprang up from behind it and gave him a heavy blow with a gun. Joseph turned around and knocked him down, then ran at the top of his speed. About half a mile farther he was attacked again in the same manner as before; he knocked this man down in like manner as the former and ran on again; and before he reached home he was assaulted the third time. In striking the last one, he dislocated his thumb, which, however, he did not notice until he came within sight of the house, when he threw himself down in the corner of the fence in order to recover his breath. As soon as he was able, he arose and came to the house. He was still altogether speechless from fright and the fatigue of running.[237]

In examining a purported history of any event, and especially when this event is questioned as to its probability, one must examine the narrative carefully to see if the record is authentic and credible.

Think about this story for a few moments. How many gold plates would it take to contain the full *Book of Mormon* with its five hundred and twenty-two pages? How many characters could one place per gold page of "reformed Egyptian" writing? How much would these gold plates weigh?

One Mormon scholar, whose name is Hal Hougey, considered all of these questions carefully. He consulted experts to see how many gold pages would be needed to contain the *Book of Mormon* with any known means of writing and especially Egyptian.

Then he considered how much gold weighs per ounce. When these calculations were made, the minimum weight that the gold plates would have had to have weighed would have been 200 or more pounds.

With this information let's run through the story again. Joseph went to the rotten birch log where he had

---

[237] *History of Joseph Smith by His Mother Lucy Smith,* pp. 107-108.

hidden the gold plates, took them out and tucked all 200 pounds of them under one arm.

He jumped over a "large windfall" and then with one hand and while carrying 200 pounds in the other, after being struck a heavy blow, he disabled the first man. He then ran on at full speed and fought that man, or another man again. The second and third men he fought were almost certainly different men because the account says, "In striking the last one . . ." indicating that there was a succession of men.

So, it seems, with 200 pounds under one arm, Joseph had run and jumped a large log, fought and beat three men, while having run three miles.

It is very unlikely that even the best of prize fighters could whip three men after having run three miles at the "top of his speed," especially while carrying 200 pounds under his arm. As the present generation would say, "Let's get serious."

It seems incredible that Joseph would get almost home and then, after having three men chasing him, would sit down in the corner of the fence and catch his breath for some time before continuing the remainder of the way home.

This, like many of Joseph's other stories bears all the marks of having been produced by his fertile imagination. Or we could say more bluntly, a bold-faced lie.

The Mormon scholar used a replica of the gold plates, which were made out of lead to simulate the size and minimum weight of what the gold plates would have had to weigh. He offered a $1,100.00 reward in the newspaper to any man who could carry them one mile.

Several weight lifters came and tried their hand at it. One managed to carry them 75 feet before dropping them.

In an inquiry that involves our eternal destiny we must be careful to not be gullible. It is quite clear why the Latter-day Saints are ashamed of Lucy's history of her son.

It is an embarrassment that there are no gold plates. Why would Joseph Smith call the witnesses (the ones God supposedly chose) a bunch of liars and thieves? Why did the three main witnesses all leave the Mormon church? How could anyone believe that Joseph Smith carried even a small fraction of the gold plates under his arm?

The story of the gold plates is not believable.*

---

*Since the first edition of this book I am grateful to Hal Hougey who told me about the event by Robert C. Jones called "The Gold Plate Pentathlon." Hal's article, "The Gold Plate Pentathlon—Non-Event of the Year" appeared in his paper, *From Moroni with Love*.

The "Gold Plates" were made by Arthur Budvarsen (now deceased) who had calculated the weight of the plates to have been at least 234 pounds. The Pentathlon events were 50-yard hurdles, 50-yard "hit-and-run," 100-yard dash, broad jump, and a three-mile run. Contestants were required to carry facsimiles of the Gold Plates under one arm, as Joseph Smith is said to have done. The contestant who completed all five events with the best overall score would receive a cash prize of $1100.

Craig Rogers of Hayward, California, was a body builder. He managed to carry the plates for 75 feet in the 50-yard hurdle event before putting them down. However, he was unable to put them under one arm; he was unable to run; and he could not go over the hurdles. It was only with great effort that he could carry the plates on both arms at a slow pace.

CHAPTER TWENTY-TWO

Ashamed of Why and How He Died

It was a pleasant, late spring day, with blue sky and a few puffy white clouds, when we set off to Carthage, Illinois to visit the site where Joseph Smith died. I was currently in seminary and my continued interest in knowing about the early history of the Mormon church brought a sense of excitement to the trip as we started out on an excursion to Carthage and Nauvoo.

When we came to the town of Carthage, being uncertain of the location of the jail, I stopped to enquire. I soon learned that the hostility against the Mormons in Carthage has still not abated. I drove into a service station, parked, and walked over to the attendant. My words to him were, "Can you tell me how to get to the jail where Joseph Smith was shot?"

The man looked at me in such a way as for me not to have forgotten, even though it has been almost twenty years.

He said, "You a Mormon?"

To which I replied,"No!"

"I want to warn you that those guides up there will sure not give you the real low-down on what happened there!"

"Is that right?"

He looked at me again, "That sure is right. They use that place to proselyte people to their #@*!% religion and you can't believe what you've been told."

I thanked him and returned to the car. When I got in the car I said to my wife, "You'll never believe the exchange that I just had with the service station operator."

"Oh?"

And I recounted what had happened.

When we arrived at the jail we found a two-story, stone building of rather modest proportions. One writer describes the jail as being,

> . . . a stout two-story stone building with a spacious cell on the upper floor. Joseph was permitted the use of several rooms, and his friends had easy access to his presence . . . .[238]

We found office and administrative space downstairs, with a rather steep and narrow staircase to the upstairs. The second story had several rooms, one in which

---

[238] Fawn Brodie, *No Man Knows My History*, p. 389.

Hyrum died and Joseph in the other. Joseph was shot at the window where he fell out to the ground.

Several things appeared odd to me. One, that the building was no larger than it was. Second, that it was not more secure. But the thing that puzzled me most was that the guide showed us a bloodstained spot on the floor. He pointed out that this was the bloodstain from Hyrum's death.

"How could this be," I wondered, "since the building had continued to be used as a jail for many years after the incident?" Had they neglected to clean the floor all that time? "Yes," I thought, "the man at the service station was right."

Be sure to keep your mind engaged when listening to the history of what really happened to Joseph and Hyrum Smith when it is from L.D.S. sources. It is not an easy task to find the real history, but, this is the intent of this chapter. Let us begin with the words of Lucy Smith.

THE JAILING OF JOSEPH SMITH

Lucy attributes much of the trouble leading to the jailing of her boys to William Law and the printing of scurrilous things about the Saints in a local newspaper. Her account goes like this:

> About the time that John C. Bennett left Nauvoo, an election was held for the office of mayor, and Joseph, being one of the candidates, was elected to that office. I mention this fact in order to explain a circumstance that took place in the winter of 1843 and 1844, which was as follows. Joseph, in organizing the city police, remarked that, "were it not for enemies within the city, there would be no danger from foes without," adding, "If it

were not for a Brutus, I might live as long as Caesar would have lived."

Someone who suspected that Joseph alluded to William Law, went to the latter and informed him that Joseph regarded him as a Brutus; and, that it was his own opinion that he (Law) was in imminent danger . . . .[239]

Law was a wealthy convert from Canada who had grown to dislike and mistrust Joseph for many reasons that will be pointed out shortly. Lucy continues:

About this time a man by the name of Joseph Jackson, who had been in the city several months, being desirous to marry Lovina Smith, Hyrum's oldest daughter, asked her father if he was willing to receive him as a son-in-law. Being answered in the negative, he went and requested Joseph to use his influence in his favor. As Joseph refused to do that, he next applied to Law, who was our secret enemy, for assistance in stealing Lovina from her father, and from this time forth he continued seeking out our enemies, till he succeeded in getting a number to join him in a conspiracy to murder the whole Smith family. They commenced holding secret meetings, one of which was attended by a man named Eaton, who was our friend, and he exposed the plot . . . .[240]

Without a doubt these were contributing factors to the fall of Joseph Smith, but who would believe that some misunderstandings over real estate, one of Law's complaints, and over a niece's marriage were the full cause of the inner problems facing Joseph. Much that lies behind the scene is not being told.

Jackson and the apostates continued to gather strength,

---

[239] *History of Joseph Smith by His Mother Lucy Smith*, p. 320.
[240] *Ibid.*, p. 321.

till, finally, they established a printing press in our midst. Through this organ they belched forth the most intolerable and the blackest lies that were ever palmed upon a community. Being advised by men of influence and standing, to have this scandalous press removed, the city council took the matter into consideration, and finding that the law would allow them to do so, they declared it a nuisance and had it treated accordingly.

At this the apostates left the city in a great rage, swearing vengeance against Joseph and the city council, and, in fact, the whole city. They went forthwith to Carthage and got out writs for Joseph and all those who were in any wise concerned in the destruction of the press . . .[241]

With this the apostates were not satisfied. They then called upon one Levi Williams, who was a bitter enemy to us, wherever he was sufficiently sober to know his own sentiments, for he was a drunken, ignorant, illiterate brute that never had a particle of character or influence until he began to call mob meetings and placed himself at the head of a rabble like unto himself, to drive the "Mormons," at which time he was joined by certain unmentionable ones in Warsaw and Carthage; and for his zeal in promoting mobocracy he became the intimate acquaintance and confidential friend of some certain preachers, lawyers, and representatives, and finally, of Joseph Jackson and the apostates . . . .[242]

A warrant was then made for Joseph and Hyrum's arrest and they were taken to Carthage jail.

My sons were thrown into jail, where they remained three days in company with Brothers Richards, Taylor and Markham. At the end of this time, the Governor disbanded most of the men, but left a guard of eight of our bitterest enemies over the jail, and sixty more of the

---

[241] *Ibid.*, p. 322.
[242] *Ibid.*

221

same character about a hundred yards distant. He then came into Nauvoo with a guard of fifty or sixty men, made a short speech, and returned immediately. During his absence from Carthage, the guard rushed Brother Markham out of the place at the point of the bayonet. Soon after this two hundred of those discharged in the morning rushed into Carthage, armed and painted black, red and yellow, and in ten minutes fled again, leaving my sons murdered and mangled corpses![243]

It would be unusual to expect a mother to give a much different report of such events. It would also be naive to suppose that this is all of the story, even as Lucy herself knew it. It would be even more gullible to suppose she truly knew the more scurrilous things that her sons had done. People are hesitant to tell mothers such things about their children.

Let's see if we can dig a bit deeper and find out more fully why people like William Law and others who had been loyal followers became so violently disaffected?

Although most Mormons have little appreciation of Fawn Brodie's book, *No Man Knows My History*, it is hard to discount much of what she says because of her elaborate footnoting and quoting from primary church sources. Few other writers have had as much access to the church archives as this niece of the then living prophet.

She may have touched on the real reasons why William Law and others were so angry.

In the beginning Law hid his resentment over the prophet's monopoly of the management of real estate in and about the city, though he thought it unseemly in a

---

man of God. He had been particularly shocked when Joseph threatened to excommunicate any wealthy convert who came to Nauvoo and purchased land without his counsel. Finally he came to mistrust Joseph's business judgment and refused to invest money in the publication of the revised version of the Bible, placing his funds instead in a steam mill and hemp farm.[244]

But there was much more to the ill will that grew between Joseph Smith and William Law.

The rift between William Law and the prophet thus began in a fundamental divergence of economic attitudes. The final break in their friendship, however, came from a question, not of finance, but of fidelity. With sorrow and suspicion Law watched Joseph ever enlarging his circle of wives. Then the prophet tried to approach Law's own wife, Jane. Denison L. Harris and Robert Scott, who spied for Joseph at the meetings held by Law and Foster, reported many years later that they had seen three veiled women, one of them William Law's wife, come to one meeting and sign affidavits to the effect that "Joseph and Hyrum Smith had endeavored to seduce them; had made the most indecent and wicked proposals to them, and wished them to become their wives."[245]

Thomas Ford also reported that Joseph attempted to win Jane Law for his wife. (See his *History of Illinois*, p. 322).[246]

We might discount these two witnesses, but there is another who gives his testimony as if from his deathbed. John

---

[244] *History of the Church*, Vol. 6, 164-5. Fawn Brodie, *No Man Knows My History*, p. 368.

[245] As reported to Horace Cummings, who described their accounts in the *Contributor*, Salt Lake City, April 1884, Vol. V, p. 255.

[246] *Ibid.*, p. 369.

D. Lee in his book *Mormonism Unveiled* says:

> A difference arose between Joseph and Wm. Law, his
> second counselor, on account of Law's wife. Law said
> that the Prophet proposed making her his wife, and she
> so reported to her husband. Law loved his wife and was
> devoted to her, as she was an amiable and handsome
> woman, and he did not feel like giving her up to anoth-
> er man. He exposed the Prophet, and from that time
> became his enemy. His brother, Wilson Law, sided with
> him. They were Canadians, and wealthy and influential
> men. They, in connection with Foster and Higbee, who
> were on the wane in the faith, established a paper at
> Nauvoo, called the Expositor, in which they took about the
> same position that the Salt Lake Daily Tribune does . . . .[247]

So Law and the *Expositor* had much more serious reasons for anger towards the prophet. The prophet had
been seeking an adulterous relationship with his lovely
wife. Lucy never knew the real reasons, nor did most of
the rest of the Mormons.[248]

> Hiram Kimball was almost ready to join their ranks . . .
> Kimball, like Law, was further embittered by jealousy,
> since Joseph had once coveted his wife, Sarah, and had
> tried in 1842 to win her for a spiritual wife. (See Sarah

---

[247] John D. Lee, *Mormonism Unveiled*, p. 147.

[248] Another report that I have read related to this same time
period. It told of a man on a two-year mission who on his
return found his wife with a newborn child. This child was
under one year. He knew it could not have been his own, so
he inquired as to who had been seen with his wife. It was
none other than the prophet.

Upon closer observation, he found the child bore a remarkable resemblance to Joseph Smith. He divorced her and she
later became the wife of Joseph Smith. This report must be
relegated to hearsay at this point, as I have been unable to
locate the source.

Kimball's sworn statement, pg. 306).[249]

Chief among the dissenters was Dr. Robert D. Foster, whose own grievances strikingly paralleled those of Kimball and William Law. For a long time had resented the prophet's opposition to his business ventures, but still looked to him for guidance in spiritual matters. Then one day in the spring of 1844 he arrived home unexpectedly from a business trip to discover the prophet dining with his wife. When Joseph left and Foster demanded to know the propose of his coming, Mrs. Foster refused to talk. Quick to anger and inordinately jealous, he drew his pistol and threatened to shoot her if she did not divulge everything the prophet had said. Gray and terrified, the woman still was silent.[250]

These, along with hundreds of other infractions had so infuriated the people of a three-state area that Mormons were in serious trouble.

Once more the Mormon women braced themselves for the shock of an uprooting. They were used to it by now, some having made all five migrations, and accepted what threatened to be expulsion from Nauvoo almost with resignation . . . .[251]

The event that brought things to a climax was the burning of the newspaper, the *Expositor*.

When Thomas Ford learned of the burning of the Expositor, he went directly to Carthage for an investigation, determined to call out the militia if necessary to bring the offenders to justice. He was appalled to discover the militia already assembling under the orders of he local constables and openly preparing for an attack on Nauvoo. After an interview with the Laws, Foster, and Hig-

---

[249] *No Man Knows My History*, p. 370.
[250] *Ibid.*, p. 371.
[251] *Ibid.*, p. 380.

bees, who, it may be assumed told him the worst, Ford wrote to the prophet demanding that he and everyone else implicated in the destruction of the Expositor submit immediately to the Carthage constable and come to that city for trial.[252]

Joseph's response was not immediate. He realized the serious nature of the events and had a feeling of impending doom and did cross the river to Iowa in a flood and storm. He started to escape for his life and then, through the pleadings of his wife Emma (by letter), and others including Hyrum, decided to face the charges and hope he would be exonerated.

The final decision was made, not by Joseph, but by Hyrum.

> Joseph now turned to his brother. "You are the oldest, Hyrum, what shall we do?"

> Hyrum, who had none of Joseph's prescience and had always believed his brother invincible, replied: "Let us go back and give ourselves up, and see the thing out."[253]

They submitted and the prisoners were taken to the Carthage jail. Here they were given the right to see emissaries from the church and were allowed to have some essential things brought to them. (Two guns were smuggled in to them).

Probably, the reason most people feared the Mormons was not grounded in their practice of polygamy, but in the realization that the Mormons were trying to rise up and take over the government.[254] People feared

---

[252] *Ibid.*, p. 382.

[253] *Ibid.*, p. 385.

[254] Nauvoo at this time was the largest city in Illinois.

that in so doing, the Mormons would take away the basic freedoms of life, such freedoms as freedom of the press. (Freedoms that Americans love, especially those in Illinois).

In jail their spirits, especially Joseph's, were very low.

> Sometime after dinner we sent for some wine. It has been reported by some that this was taken as a sacrament. It was no such thing; our spirits were generally dull and heavy, and it was sent for to revive us. I think it was Captain Jones who went after it, but they would not suffer him to return. I believe we all drank of the wine, and gave some to one or two of the prison guards. We all of us felt unusually dull and languid, with a remarkable depression of spirits. In consonance with those feelings I sang a song, that had lately been introduced into Nauvoo, entitled, "A Poor Wayfaring Man of Grief," etc.[255]

Joseph paid for the wine.

THE DEATH OF JOSEPH SMITH

What happened next is reported in several different ways. We might have a tendency to believe the account as given in the *History of the Church* if so many efforts to correct and change history had not been so frequently used by the church and the three accounts given in Volume six and seven to be at variance.

Volume six says:

> The guard immediately sent for a bottle of wine, pipes, and two small papers of tobacco; and one of the guards

---

[255] *History of the Church*, Vol. 7, p. 101.

brought them into the jail soon after the jailer went out. Dr. Richards uncorked the bottle, and presented a glass to Joseph, who tasted, as also Brother Taylor and the doctor, and the bottle was then given to the guard, who turned to go out. When at the top of the stairs some one below called him two or three times, and he went down.

Immediately there was a little rustling at the outer door of the jail, and a cry of surrender, and also a discharge of three or four firearms followed instantly. The doctor glanced an eye by the curtain of the window, and saw about a hundred armed men around the door.

It is said that the guard elevated their firelocks, and boisterously threatening the mob discharged their firearms over their heads. The mob encircled the building, and some of them rushed by the guard up the flight of stairs, burst open the door, and began the work of death, while others fired in through the open windows.

In the meantime Joseph, Hyrum, and Elder Taylor had their coats off. Joseph sprang to his coat for his six-shooter, Hyrum for his single barrel, Taylor for Markham's large hickory cane, and Dr. Richards for Taylor's cane. All sprang against the door, the balls whistled up the stairway, and in an instant one came through the door.

Joseph Smith, John Taylor and Dr. Richards sprang to the left of the door, and tried to knock aside the guns of the ruffians.

Hyrum was retreating back in front of the door and snapped his pistol, when a ball struck him in the left side of his nose, and he fell on his back on the floor saying, "I am a dead man!" As he fell on the floor another ball from the outside entered his left side, and passed through his body with such force that it completely broke to pieces the watch he wore in his vest pocket, and at the same instant another ball from the door grazed his breast, and entered his head by the throat; subsequently a fourth ball entered his left leg.

A shower of balls was pouring though all parts of the room, many of which lodged in the ceiling just above the head of Hyrum.

Joseph reached round the door casing, and discharged his six-shooter into the passage, some barrels missing fire . . . .[256]

The church history repeats the story of Joseph discharging his six-shooter down the stairway.

Joseph, seeing there was no safety in the room, and no doubt thinking that it would save the lives of his brethren in the room if he could get out, turned calmly from the door, dropped his pistol on the floor, and sprang into the window when two balls pierced him from the door, and one entered his right breast from without, and he fell outward into the hands of his murderers, exclaiming, "O Lord, my God!"[257]

Fawn Brodie tells the story from a somewhat different point of view, but the essence is quite similar.

Joseph had a six-shooter and Hyrum a single-barrel pistol, which had been smuggled in by friends the previous day. The other two men had nothing to defend themselves with save two hickory canes. All four sprang against the door, but retreated when the first ball penetrated the thick panel.

As the door was forced open, three of the prisoners jumped nimbly to the left. But Hyrum was caught by fire from one of the half-dozen muzzles pointed evilly towards the doorway. The first ball struck him in the nose and he stumbled backward crying: "I am a dead man!" As he was falling, three more caught him from

---

[256] *History of the Church*, Vol. 6, pp. 617-618.
[257] *Ibid.*, p. 618.

the door, and a fourth ball from the window shattered his left side.

Joseph now discharged all six barrels down the passage-way. Three of them missed fire, but the other three found marks. One of the wounded rushed back down the stairs, his arm a mass of blood and mangled flesh. "Are you badly hurt?" someone shouted.

"Yes, my arm is all shot to pieces by Old Joe," he screamed, "but I don't care; I've got revenge; I shot Hyrum!"

A shower of balls was now pouring into the room. John Taylor was hit five times, but the only bullet that might have killed him struck his watch, which was in his vest pocket, and was deflected harmless away. Willard Richards, who was as big a man as Joseph, miraculously escaped being hit at all, save for a ball that slightly grazed his throat and ear lobe, although he stood close to the door beating vainly at the guns with his cane. Most of the balls coming in through the window were striking harmlessly against the ceiling, while the men in the hallway who had not been hit or frightened back by Joseph's shooting were trying to fix their aim upon him.

When his pistol was empty, Joseph flung it on the floor crying: "There, defend yourselves as well as you can," and sprang to the window. He looked out upon a hundred bayonets gleaming dully in the murky light that seeped through the heavy storm clouds. Behind every bayonet there was a hideously painted face, and it must have seemed to him as if hell itself had vomited up this apparition.

It is said by some who saw him that he gave the Masonic signal of distress and cried out: "Is there no help for the widow's son?" Then a ball from the door caught him in the back and he pitched slowly forward out of the window, his hands still gripping the sill from which he had been preparing to jump. For an instant he hung to the sill swinging, while Levi Williams, the colonel commanding the Warsaw militia, shouted: "Shoot him! God damn him! Shoot the damned rascal!"

But no one shot. William Daniels, who was standing petrified at the sight, heard him cry: "Oh Lord, my God!" and watched him drop to the ground. He twisted as he fell, landing on his right shoulder and back, and then rolled over on his face. One of the militia, bare footed and bareheaded, grinning through his black paint, leaped forward and dragged him against the well-curb in the yard.

The prophet stirred a little and opened his eyes. . . . Colonel Williams now ordered four men to fire at him. As the balls struck he cringed a little and fell forward on his face.[258]

The official history of the church brings out one more view of these events and also causes us to wonder if any of those who edit these books ever read them carefully. For it tells quite a different story of Joseph's last few moments of life.

When the jail in Carthage was assailed, and the mob was pouring murderous volleys into the room occupied by himself and friends, the Prophet turned from the prostrate form of his murdered brother to face death-dealing guns and bravely returned the fire of his assailants, "bringing his man down every time," and compelling even John Hay, who but reluctantly accords the Prophet any quality of virtue, to confess that he "made a handsome fight" in the jail.[259]

---

[258] *No Man Knows My History,* pp. 393-394.
[259] *History of the Church,* Vol. 6, Introduction p. XLI.

A footnote on that page gives us additional information as to who was shot and what kinds of wounds they received.

> *This is the late Secretary of State John Hay, in the Atlantic Monthly for December 1869; Joe Smith died bravely, he stood by the jam of the door and fired four shots, bringing his man down every time. He shot an Irishman named Wills who was in the affair from his congenital love of a brawl, in the arm; Gallagher, a Southerner from the Mississippi bottom, in the face; Voorhees, a half-grown hobbledehoy from Bear Creek, in the shoulder; and another gentleman, whose name I will not mention, as he is prepared to prove an alibi, and besides stands six feet two in his moccasins.[260]

John Taylor, one of the persons present, said of this event,

> . . . I afterwards understood that two or three were wounded by these discharges, two of whom, I am informed, died. I had in my hands a large strong hickory stick . . . .[261]

Do you recall what the church has always said about Joseph Smith? "A better man never lived." The message always has been that Joseph Smith died as a martyr for truth and holiness. So often the missionaries have told me, "He died just like Jesus."

Unfortunately history paints a completely different story and this story is not given by unreliable witnesses, but by people who were first-hand witnesses, people on the scene, people who lived out the events, people who

---

[260] *Ibid.*, footnote, Introduction p. XLI.
[261] *Ibid.*, Vol. 7, pp. 102-103.

suffered because of the ill advised leading of their prophet. This account is written in the approved *History of the Church.*

Joseph was in jail because of his own sins committed against those closest to him, men and women who had his trust; people who truly believed he was a prophet of God.

It was these people he betrayed and seduced. One witness might be overlooked as a crank or liar, but when there are numerous witnesses who claim Joseph tried to seduce or did seduce their wives, they cannot be disregarded. These men were of the highest echelons of power in the Mormon system.

I can hardly stomach even one more person comparing Joseph Smith to Jesus Christ, or for that matter to Elijah, Elisha, Isaiah, Jeremiah or John the Baptist. These were good, honest, moral, nonviolent people.

Joseph was a proven womanizer, violent man of blood and brutality. He did not die a martyr. He died defending himself with his last bullet and ounce of strength. He shot the other men, not to defend Hyrum (he was already dead), but in pure self-defense.

How can he be compared with humble Jesus who patiently endured pain and suffering, being able to call all the angels of heaven in His defense, but He did not. Instead He suffered quietly, with dignity, and with every evidence that He was what He claimed.

Joseph, rather, died in a battle from which he had tried to run away. He was ready to raise the militia. Yes, he did show bravery, but not the marks of a true prophet of God.

It is no wonder that the Latter-day Saints are ashamed of Joseph's mother's history and the facts surrounding his death.

Yes, it was probably murder, but not martyrdom.

CONCLUSION

*The conclusion,
when all has been heard, is:
fear God and keep His commandments,
because this applies to every person.*

Ecclesiastes 12:13

*So teach us to number our days,
that we may present to Thee
a heart of wisdom.*

Psalms 90:12

CHAPTER TWENTY-THREE

A Summary of Embarrassments

It is little wonder that the Latter-day Saints are embarrassed by the life of Joseph Smith, their prophet. People who know the facts of his life will not become converts.

There is growing evidence that the church is trying to downplay those things in their history of which they are embarrassed.

But this leaves them with a very serious problem. How can they explain the very bold pronouncements of Joseph and the succeeding prophets of their church in regard to his place of eminence?

Why, if Brigham Young was a true prophet, would he

speak so emphatically?

> Well, now examine the character of the Savior, and examine the character of those who have written the Old and New Testament; and then compare them with the character of Joseph Smith, the founder of this work . . . and you will find that his character stands as fair as that of any man's mentioned in the Bible. We can find no person who presents a better character to the world when the facts are known than Joseph Smith, Jun., the prophet . . . .[262]

Really? Was he superior in character to Abraham? Jeremiah? Elijah? John the Baptist? John the Apostle? Now really, better than Jesus Christ?

How can Brigham Young dishonor the truth as he does when he said, ". . . a better man never lived upon the face of the earth?"[263]

The words of my mother ring in my ears, "Tell the truth and shame the devil." Brigham's mother must not have told him this! Can we really accept Joseph as better than Jesus? Could anyone consider Joseph superior to the Apostle John or Paul?

With all of the well documented evidence about the sinful and proud life that Joseph Smith lived can we consider him an honest man? What should we conclude about a man who said that he was ". . . learned and know more than all the world put together?" What should we think about a man who boasted that he could comprehend, "heaven, earth, and hell" and that God Himself was his "right hand man?"[264]

---

[262] *Journal of Discourses*, Vol. 14: p. 203.

[263] *Ibid.*, Vol. 4, p. 41.

[264] *History of the Church of Jesus Christ of Latter-day Saints*, Vol. 5, p. 289 and Vol. 6, pp. 408-409.

Really, Joseph, you are a model of humility and Christian modesty. Certainly no one in your family had any ego, you got it all!

Joseph Fielding Smith, the tenth prophet and president of the Mormon church is certainly right:

> Mormonism, as it is called, must stand or fall on the story of Joseph Smith. He was either a prophet of God, divinely called, properly appointed and commissioned, or he was one of the biggest frauds this world has ever seen. There is no middle ground.

> If Joseph Smith was a deceiver, who wilfully attempted to mislead the people, then he should be exposed; his claims be refuted, and his doctrines shown to be false, for the doctrines of an imposter cannot be made to harmonize in all particulars with divine truth. If his claims and declarations were built upon fraud and deceit, there would appear many errors and contradictions, which would be easy to detect. The doctrines of false teachers will not stand the test when tried by the accepted standards of measurement, the Scriptures.[265]

Certainly he is right. We have accepted his challenge and exposed Joseph Smith for what he really was, a brilliant fraud. His teachings have never harmonized with the Bible, or for that matter even his writings—the *Book of Mormon, Doctrine and Covenants,* and *Pearl of Great Price.*

The most puzzling part of all is—why would any person of average intelligence be taken in by such giganticly erroneous statements?

We have tried Joseph Smith's claims; he has been

---

[265] *Doctrines of Salvation,* 1:188.

"weighed in the balances and found wanting."[266]

He was tried and convicted for using his seer stones to find buried treasure.

His bold story about talking to God, Jesus, and angels would have been far more convincing if he would have gotten around to telling it when it happened rather than waiting for more than two decades. His story would have been more credible if he could have told the same story repeatedly without changing important details.

If Joseph was such a godly example, an illustration of humanity at its very best—why did he have so many wives and concubines? Why did he consummate a sexual relationship with a 15-year-old girl when he had numerous other wives? Did this young girl not have the right to her own husband? Was she not entitled to a man whom she could love and cherish instead of a man old enough to be her father, who had many other women to his credit? Can you accept such a person as your prophet?

If Joseph was one of the finest men who ever lived— why was he always in a fight? He fought with three men while retrieving the golden plates. He beat one Baptist minister till he "begged for his life." Another man he slapped till he left him blind. Does this fit the mold of the finest man who ever lived?

---

[266] Daniel 5:27

If humility is one of the eminent Christian graces— why did Joseph have himself anointed King? Why did Joseph desire to become General of his army? Why would he run for the Presidency of the United States? Why would he desire to "rule" the world?

If Joseph was such a paragon of virtue and wisdom— why did he organize "The Whittlers," who later became "The Avenging Angels," and finally "The Danites?" Why would godly prophets keep a thug around like Bill Hickman, a man who cut off another man's head and carried it home behind his saddle for a $100.00 reward? Why would a system of truth and godliness have a man who would take a prisoner in leg irons and while he was asleep chop him to death with an ax?

If Joseph were such an honest prophet—why did all of his prophecies fail? Who could believe that he was anything more than a cunning fraud? Can you accept a man as a prophet of God who said the moon was populated by men who dressed like Quakers and lived to be one thousand years old?

If Joseph were such a model of excellence—why did his bank fail and so many people lose hundreds of thousands of dollars, never to regain their money? Couldn't this be one of the reasons Mormons were driven from the various places they lived?

If his writings were the very works of God and the most accurate works ever published by men—why did the *Book of Mormon* have seven mistakes on each side of each page? Why did the *Doctrine and Covenants* have over 2,786 words changed and twenty-one doctrinal changes?

Why are church leaders so ashamed of his mother's history of Joseph? Why does this history show that the family had been involved in spiritism and the occult? Why did Brigham Young, second prophet of the church, have to threaten excommunication for those who even had a copy of it?

If Joseph Smith was a true prophet—why is there proof that two (or more) people wrote books very similar to the *Book of Mormon* years before he did? Who wrote first, Ethan Smith? Solomon Spaulding? Certainly not Joseph Smith. Joseph was at least five, and maybe ten years (or several hundred) too late.

If the *Book of Mormon* is so ancient—why are there so many cities of very recent origin, with the same names and proximity to each other as those mentioned in his gold bible, and yet in a very different part of the country from where the events were supposed to have taken place? The only reasonable answer is that he was a charlatan and worthy of shame.

How could Joseph Smith be considered a prophet when he taught so many irrational and Bible contradicting things? How can we believe anything Joseph said when so much of it is diametrically opposed to the Bible?

If Joseph, the prophet, spoke on behalf of God—why did so much he wrote contradict the *Book of Mormon*? If he was here to represent a renewed and restored gospel—why is it riddled with mistakes and why are so many people trying to deny what he certainly taught?

Even Joseph Smith's death is a matter of shame. We see Jesus and the Apostles dying as worthy martyrs, none raising up against their accusers. But Joseph killed two men and wounded a third in his death. Why did he call out the masonic signal of distress if his trust was truly in God?

Is there a need to say anything more? Has not the case been clearly made that Joseph Smith was not a prophet of God, but a liar, fornicator, impostor, and false prophet? Hasn't our case been substantiated when we learn that Joseph died at age thirty-nine in a gun battle because he had violated the most sacred trusts of friendship and morality? Doesn't it speak to Joseph's true nature when we realize that he died because people from within his own ranks rose up in dismay and disgust against him? Isn't it troubling to find that the rebellion against Joseph was led by three former friends whose wives Joseph had tried to seduce?

The church has every reason to be ashamed of him. He is indefensible. If there are true men of God in this church called Mormonism, they need to stand up and with clarion call, beseech people to leave this religious system and follow the real Jesus of the Bible.

In forty years of dealing with the Latter-day Saints of

243

all levels of authority (even their present prophet), not once have I found a person able to defend their doctrine. Never in public or private has there ever been a person who has successfully refuted the problems posed in this book. NOT ONE! Mormonism is an indefensible cancer on all that is holy or called Christian.

CHAPTER TWENTY-FOUR

Christians Need To Be Embarrassed

After such a study the tendency might be to feel a little smug about our own better judgment in our search for truth. We may be like the person used in one of the parables of Jesus.

> The Pharisee stood and was praying thus to himself, "God, I thank Thee that I am not like other people: swindlers, unjust, adulterers, or even like this tax-gatherer . . . ."[267]

Is our responsibility fulfilled to God by simply knowing the truth? Do we not need to feel concern for and a desire to help our Mormon friends and neighbors?

---

[267] Luke 18:11

Remember the words of Jesus:

Jesus replied and said, "A certain man was going down from Jerusalem to Jericho; and he fell among robbers, and they stripped him and beat him, and went off leaving him half dead. And by chance a certain priest was going down on that road, and when he saw him he passed by on the other side. And likewise a Levite also, when he came to the place and saw him, passed by on the other side. But a certain Samaritan, who was on a journey, came upon him; and when he saw him, he felt compassion, and came to him, and bandaged up his wounds, pouring oil and wine on them; and he put him on his own beast, and brought him to an inn, and took care of him. And on the next day he took out two denarii and gave them to the innkeeper and said, 'Take care of him; and whatever more you spend, when I return, I will repay you.' Which of these three do you think proved to be a neighbor to the man who fell into the robber's hands?"[268]

All around us are those who have fallen into the hands of the religious charlatans. They have been robbed of truth and heaven. They have been left in a case of spiritual death.

What has the church in general done? We have turned our backs and passed along on the other side of the road. What has been the general response to the inroads of the missionaries into the midst of many congregations? The Christians just let them be led away into falsehood. This usually happens because of our ignorance. We do not know how to defend the faith.

Yes, the number one source of converts to Mormonism is from Protestant churches. Many Catholics

---

[268] Luke 10:30-36

are won. The most fertile field of endeavor for the Latter-day Saints is found among those who are already church members.

This condition must be stopped. During thirty years of ministry only one person from the church I served was ever led away into Mormonism. That happened while I was away for a month, out of the country.

Upon my return the church said in despair that one of our lonely young divorcees had been baptized into the Mormon church. I immediately went to her home with one of our deacons.

When questioned she said, "I was so lonely and they gave me what I needed."

My reply to her was, "Haven't we helped you by praying with you, counseling you and helping you with food and your bills?"

She replied, "But you didn't give me what I needed most."

I asked, "And what was that?"

She said, "I needed someone to put their arms around me and give me love and affection. They have done that for me."

I said, "Do I understand what you are saying to me?"

She replied, "I think so; the ward teacher has spent three nights with me, and so have each of the missionaries."

I asked, "In bed!!!?"

She replied, "Yes."

The deacon and I addressed the subject of adultery, stressing that the ward teacher was married and she was not married to the missionaries.

The very next Sunday she came to confess that she had sinned and asked God and the congregation to forgive her for being led away by false teachers.

This is not to suggest that this is a common practice of Latter-day Saints ward teachers or missionaries. But it is to illustrate that in over 35 years, not one member from a congregation I have served, has really been led into Mormonism.

During this same time period, about 300 Mormons have been taught out of their false system and have come to place their trust in the real Jesus and have been baptized into Him.

This is what should be happening, rather than just turning our backs when the person begins to study with some cultish group. When that happens it presents a wonderful opportunity for you to lead the cultish member to Christ.

But if that is to happen you will need to become prepared, well prepared! This will take a lot of time. Most churches have found that one or more members are interested in the subject of the cults already. If they will become specialists they can care for this specialized ministry.

There needs to be a change of attitude from fear and retreat to loving militancy. This means that we need to press our missionary efforts towards leading them to Christ the Lord.

In our experience we have found them some of the more easily won people. There are so many errors that are readily demonstrated and without a great investment of time and research. No other one religious body has contributed more conversions in the years of my ministry.

You might answer, "But you are an expert." No, this is not the reason. People have been won consistently from the very beginning when my knowledge was very inadequate.

What is the basic element? Love for these fine people—a desire to reach out to them in friendship, a willingness to enter into discussions about our mutual faith, and an earnest desire to serve God with your own life. I firmly believe that if you can start a Mormon thinking, you are half way to bringing them out of Mormonism.

If you are interested in learning more, I would suggest as a very primary tool in winning Mormons to Christ, my book, *The Bible and Mormon Scriptures Compared*. The subtitle of this book illustrates its purpose: "The Educational Process of Leading a Mormon to Christ."

Mormonism (only a caricature of true Christianity) must be exposed for its true nature and teaching. The eight million people who now lay spiritually wounded and bleeding by the wayside need to have their spiritual wounds medicated, bound up and healed.

It is past time for Christians everywhere to speak up for their faith. What we have to offer is Jesus the Living Word, known to us by the written word the Bible.

The Holy Bible gives us a safe and sure revelation of God, Christ and what They expect of us to find eternal salvation.

Submitting to Jesus makes one a Christian!

Submitting to Jesus plus Joseph Smith makes one a Mormon.

If it takes Jesus plus anyone else to save you then Jesus cannot save at all. It is to admit that Jesus was not the Savior of mankind.

Salvation is not Jesus plus anything. It is not Jesus plus Dr. Crane, Jesus plus Mohammed, Jesus plus some worldwide church leader, or Jesus plus Joseph Smith.

The Bible says, speaking of Jesus Christ:

> And there is salvation in no one else; for there is no other name under heaven that has been given among men, by which we must be saved.[269]

Are the Mormons ashamed of Joseph Smith? Yes, and well they should be! On the other hand, we have no reason to be ashamed of our faith.

> For I am not ashamed of the gospel, for it is the power of God for salvation to every one who believes, to the Jew first and also to the Greek.[270]

Can we know we are saved? Certainly. If we in faith submit in obedience to Jesus we are saved! I am so grateful for a personal relationship with the real Jesus on the basis of His Divine Word, the Holy Bible. For this no person need be ashamed. Amen.

---

[269] Acts 4:12
[270] Romans 1:16

Appendix

Further Evidence

The media is filled with advertisements for the L.D.S. church. These presentations do not even hint at the true nature of the Mormon religion.

Over Christmas break one of our professors called and requested a copy of a video that promised to give a clear picture of the L.D.S. church. When it came, I viewed it and found further confirmation of the basic premise of this book. Not one word was mentioned about their founding prophet Joseph Smith. Several things stood out in my mind while viewing this video.

Why was nothing said about their founding prophet,

Joseph Smith? Was he not supposed to be better than anyone else in the Bible? Was he not equal to, if not greater than, Jesus Himself? Why not even mention the one to whom God appeared, who translated their golden Bible, who gave most of the *Doctrine and Covenants* and the *Pearl of Great Price*?

In contrast, the Old Testament prophets, Elijah and Elisha are mentioned in the video. The New Testament prophets are referred to as well as the living prophets that guide their church today—but there is not one word about Joseph Smith.

Why do they not utter a single word about the founder and writer of the major part of their whole religious system? Why? They are becoming increasingly more ashamed of Joseph Smith. He is indefensible.

The video is called, "Our Heavenly Father's Plan." Unfortunately the plan is not our Heavenly Father's plan nor is it in harmony with the teachings given by Jesus and His Apostles. It is a highly romanticized plan, based not on truth, but on the teachings of the very person of whom they are justifiably ashamed, Joseph Smith.

If you were to watch the L.D.S. video program, you might make an observation that has often troubled me. When the Mormons "bear their testimony" they get a far off look in their eyes. They will not make eye contact, but gaze off into space. They look rather mindless or robotic.

It reminds me of a fellow I knew as a kid. He was always concocting some outlandish story. We all felt sorry for him because he would rather lie than tell the truth. When he told his stories he would get this same look on his face. It was as if he was possessed by some other spirit. I perceive the Mormon missionaries in this same way.

I find the video to be about as truthful as a real estate salesman peddling swamp land from the Everglades. It is nothing more than an appeal by the Church of Jesus Christ of Latter-day Saints to be accepted as mainstream Christianity. In reality, they are farther from being truly Christian than is the Islamic religion. Certainly Islam has a more correct teaching about God, Christ and the Bible than they do.

"Beware of the false prophet who comes in sheep's clothing." False prophets do not announce their true nature, but rather want to look like sheep, smell like sheep, and bleat like lambs. The Bible calls such a person what they ought to be called, a wolf.

The Latter-day Saints are trying (for good reason) to downplay Joseph Smith's role in their religion.

The Author's Interest

As a boy of 14, I was walking on the back part of our ranch in the beautiful Cascade Mountains of Oregon. I heard a caterpillar tractor coming over a rise and saw it was pulling a large log.

My first thought was that someone was stealing timber off of our ranch. I walked toward the cat and observed that it looked like it was brand new. It stopped and one of the most handsome men I had ever seen got off. He kept his equipment as well as he did himself.

He pulled off his glove and stuck out his hand and said, "My name is Homer Moxley." He was clean and looked like he had just come out of a men's store.

He quickly told me that my father had given him permission to yard some logs across the back part of our ranch. We became good friends from the very first moment.

Later that year I worked for him on his ranch building fence and putting up hay. I soon learned that he belonged to the Latter-day Saints and he gave me my very first *Book of Mormon*.

We had several discussions about their religion and it was not long before Homer was baptized into Christ and has been a very faithful Christian all these years. He has had a very good influence in my life.

From that time forward I became interested in the study of L.D.S. writings, doctrines and history. I have tried to read their primary documents and study whatever I could find.

For seven and one half years we lived in Salt Lake

City and during those days I studied with every Mormon person who would spend time with me. I have discussed these issues with some of the leading defenders of the the Mormon faith. These talks have even included a breakfast meeting with their present prophet, Ezra Taft Benson.

It has been with pleasure that I have observed my youngest son, Steven, take up this study. He recently taught a series of lessons on the cults and I had the privilege to listen and learn. When I recognized his expertise, I asked if he would assist me in the preparation of this book. He has been a tremendous help. He has not only added a wealth of information to this book, but has added to its quality as well. The book, therefore, bears both of our names.

Steve Crane

Bibliography

BOOKS

Adair, James. *The History of the American Indians.* London: Edward and Charles Dilly, 1775.

Ankerberg, John and John Weldon. *Everything You Ever Wanted to Know About Mormonism.* Eugene: Harvest House Publishers, 1992.

Benson, Ezra Taft. *The Teachings of Ezra Taft Benson.* Salt Lake City: Bookcraft, 1988.

Berrett, William E. *The Restored Church.* Salt Lake City: Deseret, 1956.

Boudinot, Elias. *A Star in the West,* or A Humble Attempt to Discover the Long Lost Tribes of Israel. Trenton: D. Fenton, S. Hutchinson, and J. Dunham, 1816.

Brodie, Fawn M. *No Man Knows My History: The Life of Joseph Smith.* 2nd ed., rev. New York: Alfred Knopf, 1971.

Bushman, Richard L. *Joseph Smith and the Beginnings of Mormonism.* Chicago: University of Illinois Press, 1984.

Cowan, Marvin W. *Mormon Claims Answered.* Published by author, 1975.

Cowdery, Wayne L., Howard A. Davis, and Donald R. Scales. *Who Really Wrote the Book of Mormon?* Santa Ana, CA: Vision House, 1977.

Crane, Charles. *The Bible and Mormon Scriptures Compared.* Joplin, MO: College Press, 1992.

Crawford, Charles. *An Essay upon the Propagation of the Gospel.* 2nd edition, Philadelphia: J. Gales, 1801.

Fraser, Gordon H. *Is Mormonism Christian?* Chicago: Moody Press, 1977.

——————. *Joseph and the Golden Plates.* Eugene: Industrial Litho, Inc., 1978.

Garcia, Gregorio. *Origen de los Indios del Nuevo Mundo, e Indias Occidentales.* Valencia: Pedro Patricio Mey, 1607.

Harrison, G.T. *That Mormon Book: Mormonism's Keystone Exposed or The Hoax Book.* By the author, 1981.

Hickman, Bill. *Brigham's Destroying Angel: Being the Life, Confession and Startling Disclosures of the Notorious Bill Hickman,* Salt Lake City: Shepard Book Company, 1904.

Holley, Vernal. *Book of Mormon Authorship: A Closer Look.* Ogden, UT: Zenos Publications, 1983.

Howe, Eber D. *History of Mormonism.* Painesville, OH: published by the author, 1840.

_____. *Mormonism Unveiled.* Painesville, Ohio: E.D. Howe, 1834.

Jenson, Andrew. *The Historical Record.* Salt Lake City: 1886-90.

Jonas, Larry. *Mormonism Claims Examined.* Grand Rapids: Baker Book House, 1961.

Kingsborough, Lord. *Antiquities of Mexico.* Seven Volumes. London: Augustine Aglio, 1830.

Lee, John D. *Confessions of John D. Lee.* Original Ed. 1878.

Martin, Walter. *The Kingdom of the Cults,* Limited Ed. Minneapolis: Bethany House Publishers, 1992.

_____. *The Maze of Mormonism.* Rev. ed. Santa Ana, CA: Vision House, 1978.

McConkie, Bruce R. *Doctrines of Salvation*. Salt Lake City: Bookcraft, 1954.

_____ . *Mormon Doctrine*. Salt Lake City: Bookcraft, 1966.

McElveen, Floyd C. *The Mormon Illusion*. Ventura, CA: Regal Books, 1983.

McKay, David O. *Gospel Ideals*. Salt Lake City: The Church of Jesus Christ of Latter-day Saints, 1953.

Nelson, Dee Jay. *The Joseph Smith Papyri —A Translation and Preliminary Survey*. Salt Lake City: Modern Microfilm Company, 1978.

_____ . *The Joseph Smith Papyri*, Pt. 2. Salt Lake City: Modern Microfilm Company, 1978.

New American Standard Bible. Nashville: Holman Bible Publishers, 1979.

Parkin, Max. *Conflict at Kirtland: A Study of the Nature and Causes of External and Internal Conflict of the Mormons in Ohio Between 1830 and 1838*. Salt Lake City: Max Parkin, 1966. Originally a thesis, Brigham Young University, 1966.

Pratt, Orson. *The Seer.* Washington, D.C.: 1853-54, Photoreprint. Salt Lake City: Eugene Wagner.

Priest, Josiah. *The Wonders of Nature and Providence Displayed*. Albany: E. and E. Hosford, 1825.

Principles of the Gospel. The Church of Jesus Christ of Latter-day Saints. Salt Lake City: The Church of Jesus Christ of Latter-day Saints, 1976.

Richards, LeGrand. *A Marvelous Work and Wonder*. Salt Lake City: Deseret Book Company, 1976.

Ropp, Harry L. *The Mormon Papers*. Downers Grove, IL: InterVarsity Press, 1977.

Shook, Charles A. *True Origin of the Book of Mormon*. Cincinnati, 1914.

Smith, Ethan. *View of the Hebrews or The Tribes of Israel in America*. Poultney, VT: Smith and Shute, 1823.

Smith, Joseph, Jr. *Doctrine and Covenants*. Salt Lake City: The Church of Jesus Christ of Latter-day Saints, n.d.

——————. *Inspired Version of the Holy Scriptures*. Independence: Herald Publishing House, 1970.

——————. *The Book of Mormon*. Salt Lake City: The Church of Jesus Christ of Latter-day Saints, 1947.

——————. *Doctrine and Covenants/Pearl of Great Price*. Salt Lake City: The Church of Jesus Christ of Latter-day Saints, 1983.

——————. *The History of the Church of Jesus Christ of Latter-day Saints*. 7 vols. Salt Lake City: Deseret News, 1951.

Smith, Joseph Fielding, comp. *Gospel Doctrine: Selections from the Sermons and Writings of Joseph F. Smith*. Salt Lake City: Deseret Book Company, 1975.

_____. *Essentials in Church History*. Salt Lake City: Deseret, 1942.

_____. *Teachings of Prophet Joseph Smith*. Salt Lake City: Deseret News Press, 1977.

_____. *The Way to Perfection*. Salt Lake City: Genealogical Society of Utah, 1931.

_____. *Doctrines of Salvation*. Compiled by Bruce R. McConkie, 3 vols. Salt Lake City: Bookcraft, 1960.

Stewart, John J. *Brigham Young and His Wives*. Salt Lake City: Mercury, 1961.

Smith, Lucy Mack. *History of Joseph Smith by His Mother*. Salt Lake City: Bookcraft, 1979.

Stout, Hosea. *On the Mormon Frontier, the Diary of Hosea Stout*. Edited by Juanita Brooks. Salt Lake City: University of Utah Press, 1964. Vol. 1, 1844-1848. Vol. 2, 1848-1861.

Tanner, Jerald and Sandra Tanner. *The Changing World of Mormonism*. Chicago: Moody Press, 1980.

_____. *Joseph Smith's Successor—an Important New Document Comes to Light*. Salt Lake City: Jerald Tanner, 1981.

_____ . *Mormonism: A Study of Mormon History and Doctrine.* Clearfield, UT: Utah Evangel Press, 1962.

_____ . *Mormonism, Shadow or Reality?* Enlarged ed. Salt Lake City: Modern Microfilm Company, 1972.

_____ . *The First Vision Examined.* Salt Lake City: Modern Microfilm Company, 1969.

The New Schaff-Herzog Encyclopedia of Religious Knowledge. 13 vols. Grand Rapids: Baker Book House, 1957.

Walters, Wesley P. *New Light on Mormon Origins from the Palmyra (NY) Revival.* Salt Lake City: Modern Microfilm Company., 1967.

_____ . *Joseph Smith Among the Egyptians.* Salt Lake City: Modern Microfilm Company, 1973.

_____ . *Joseph Smith's Bainbridge, N.Y. Court Trial.* Salt Lake City: Modern Microfilm Company, 1977.

Whitmer, David. *An Address to All Believers in Christ.* Richmond, MO: David Whitmer, 1887.

Widtsoe, John A. *Joseph Smith-Seeker After Truth.* Salt Lake City: Bookcraft, 1951.

Wood, Wilford C. *Joseph Smith Begins His Work: The Book of Mormon.* First Edition 1830. 2 Vols. *The Book of Commandments,* i.e., The *Doctrine and Covenants,* First Edition. Published by Wilford C. Wood, 1958.

Worsley, Israel. *A View of the American Indians.* London: R. Hunter, 1828.

Young, Brigham. *Journal of Discourses.* 27 vols. 1966.

PAMPHLETS, BOOKLETS, AND LETTERS

Bodine, Jerry and Marian. *Whom Can You Trust?* Santa Ana, CA: Christ for the Cults, 1978.

Hansen, Klaus J. "The Theory and Practice of the Political Kingdom of God in Mormon History, 1829-1890." Master's Thesis: Brigham Young University, typed copy: 1959.

Smithsonian Institution, Department of Anthropology. "Statement Regarding the *Book of Mormon.*" Washington, DC: Smithsonian Institution, 1988.

Spaulding, F.S. and Samuel A.B. Mercer. *Why Egyptologists Reject the Book of Abraham.* Salt Lake City: Utah Lighthouse Ministry, n.d.

NEWSPAPER AND PERIODICAL ARTICLES

Amboy Journal. April 30, 1879 and June 11, 1879.

Brigham Young University Studies. Provo, UT: 1959-Present.

Campbell, Alexander. *The Millennial Harbinger,* Bethany, VA: February 1831.

Deseret News. Salt Lake City: 1850-Present.

Dialogue: A Journal of Mormon Thought. Arlington, VA: 1966-Present.

Evening and The Morning Star. Independence, MO: 1832-34.

Fraser's Magazine. London: February. 1873.

Juvenile Instructor. Salt Lake City: 1866-1970.

Kansas City Daily Journal. Kansas City: June 5, 1881.

Latter-Day Saints' Messenger and Advocate. 3 vols. Kirtland, OH: 1834-37.

McKay, Robert. "Joseph Smith's False Prophecies." *The Salt Lake Tribune*, n.d.

News Review. Nampa, ID: 1978.

Salt Lake Tribune. Salt Lake City: 1871-Present.

Times and Seasons. 6 vols. Nauvoo, IL: 1839-46.

U.S. News and World Report. September 28, 1992.

Utah Holiday Magazine. Salt Lake City: 1976.